The Moment of Change: WHEN DESTINY Cried AND I ANSWERED

FEATURED CO-AUTHORS:

Priscilla George, Sherito Smith, Jakia Jones, Ibadan Mack, Tara Melvin-Mack, So'leil Thompson, Tashana Howard, Tyshana Mabry-Diaz, Shauna Monroe, Kris-Shae McCall

Project Coordinator: Ebony M. Walker

Printed in the United States of America.

ISBN: 9798346611509

DEDICATION

To the movement sparked within the walls of a humble classroom, where hearts and minds aligned in unwavering faith. This book is dedicated to each of you who gathered, willing and eager to be vessels for God's Will. May the seeds planted through your dedication continue to flourish, inspiring countless others to answer the call of faith, courage, and purpose. Thank you for believing, for persevering, and for championing a vision greater than any of us alone. This is for the harvest yet to come.

Table of Contents

Acknowledgments i

Introduction by Ebony M. Walker 1

1 So'leil Thompson – *Be Aware! Who Damaged You?* 4

2 Jakia Jones – *Girl, Get Somewhere and Sit Down!* 15

3 Sherito Smith – *A Diamond that Found it Rough* 27

4 Ibadan Mack – *After the Flash* 43

5 Priscilla George – *Healing* 59

6 Tyshana Mabry-Diaz – *I Forgive Me!* 79

7 Tara Melvin-Mack – *The Coat, the Chair, and the Cave: Moments that Changed Me* 92

8 Kris-Shae McCall – *I Can See Clearly Now: The Journey to Becoming* 103

9 Tashana Howard – *Embrace Your Kairos Season* 119

10 Shauna Monroe – *The Unwavering Strength I Didn't Know I Had* 130

About the Project Coordinator 141

Acknowledgments

This book would not have been possible without the support, generosity, and dedication of so many remarkable individuals.

First, a heartfelt thank you to **Dr. Erika McCormick** of **Abundant Living Consulting** for providing her beautiful facility. Your space became a haven of inspiration and growth, and we are incredibly grateful for the atmosphere of peace and purpose that you fostered.

Our deepest gratitude to **Daniel Dricksell** and **Atreyu McLaurin** for capturing these moments with excellence and care. Your skill and attention to detail brought this moment to life, ensuring that these memories are preserved and shared in the most powerful way.

Special thanks to **Zeida Gaston** for providing delicious meals for our masterclass authors. Your culinary talent and attention to detail created an experience of warmth and hospitality that nurtured both body and spirit.

To each of you, thank you for contributing your time, talent, and heart to this project. Your dedication helped shape an environment where God's presence was truly felt and lives were changed. This book is a reflection of your selflessness and commitment, and we are forever grateful.

ANTHOLOGY PROJECT

Introduction

Birthing something meaningful and lasting is never easy, but it's always necessary. For so many of us, the dreams, ideas, and gifts that God has placed within us feel like heavy burdens—not because they aren't precious, but because we've held onto them far too long. We can't keep carrying full-grown dreams—babies, teenagers, and even adults—in our spiritual wombs. There comes a time when we must allow what's inside of us to come forth, no matter how uncomfortable the birthing process may be. It's a call to release, to step into obedience, and to let God bring purpose through us in ways we might never have expected.

This book, *The Moment of Change: When Destiny Cried and I Answered*, was born out of one such act of obedience. It started as a simple masterclass for authors, designed to help them explore new ways to use content they already had. Preparation for the event was extremely stressful, as there were so many things that I personally felt this class *had* to have...and I wanted it to be perfect for them. I had plans, I had a syllabus, I had questions and activities. And you guessed it — 90% of what I planned did not happen. Yet, 100% of what God wanted is what came to pass!

As the session unfolded, the Holy Spirit took over, turning a practical training session into a life-changing experience. I could feel it—the stirring, the tugging of something greater. While each participant was jotting down ideas of what they would call a book or a chapter about their life, a single instruction echoed in my spirit: "Create an anthology project. Position each person to tell their story and make them best-selling authors."

What happened next was nothing short of divine. This room of writers transformed into a sacred space of tears, prayers, prophetic words, and complete surrender to God's plan. One by one, these individuals embraced their unique journeys, and together, we became united by a purpose that extended beyond this class and ourselves. As each person shared their life story title, they stepped out of their comfort zones and into obedience, trusting that God was aligning the pieces of their lives in ways they least expected for this setting. Through the power of one decision—one 'yes' to God—the trajectory of lives was altered, and a legacy was born.

This book is the culmination of that obedience, a collection of stories from people who answered God's call, shared their hearts, and embraced their moments of change. Each story here represents not just a personal journey but a collective reminder that when we yield to God's timing, He will bring everything together for a purpose beyond what we could ever imagine. I pray that as you read these testimonies, you will be inspired to trust in the timing of your own God-ordained and Holy Spirit orchestrated moments, to bring forth what the Father has placed within you, and to know that your obedience has the power to change lives.

Welcome to *The Moment of Change: When Destiny Cried and I Answered.* Let each story remind you of the beauty, the power, and the purpose of walking in obedience. May this journey bless you as much as it has blessed each one of us who dared to say, "Yes, Lord."

CHAPTER 1 - SO'LEIL THOMPSON

Be Aware!
Who Damaged You?

It's always easy to point the finger at everyone else. Someone has to take the blame for the trauma I've endured, right? Imagine being the firstborn daughter to two teenagers, aged fifteen and seventeen. The story of young love, creating a beautiful child, who would later grow up to be a resilient, strong warrior. But at what cost?

Nobody talked about mental health when I was growing up. Picture being overwhelmed with anxiety and fear, with nobody to help make sense of what's going on. I have probably seen more than I should have, but I internalized everything and spent years bottling my emotions. Nobody knew the battles I fought because I masked my hurt by smiling and persevering, hoping that one day I would be something greater. I deserved greater because, after all, I didn't ask to be here. Would you believe me if I told you I was a planned pregnancy? Well, I was and my dad knew I was going to be a shining light. After all, he named me after the sun. Life forced me to embrace that fact about myself because there were times I didn't recognize my worth. It was sometimes hard for me to believe that my presence truly mattered. I remember looking forward to moving out of the house and being free, but I never really understood the cost of that choice until it was too late.

When I was sixteen, I wrote a letter to myself for teen living class. I manifested two children, a husband, and a house with a fence around the backyard. By eighteen, I was no longer living with my parents and free to create whatever life I chose. While education was supposed to be my top priority, I couldn't focus while my life was in shambles. I lost my grandfather, who had been the closest thing to me during my freshman year, and it was hard to shake back from that. I thought that college would give me a way out, but situations don't always play out how you plan them.

Juggling school with a full time job to support myself as a freshman and sophomore became overwhelming. UNCG required all students on academic probation to enroll in therapy. While I didn't find it necessary, therapy actually became a safe place for me to grow and recognize where I could improve in many areas of my life. The sessions were supposed to help us understand how our life choices were affecting our studies and so much made sense to me after that. During those sessions, I could cry, reflect, and get to the root of my distractions. After sharing my truth, the therapist recommended that I write a letter to my parents. This was challenging but a pivotal point in my healing journey because I learned to speak up and address how I felt, regardless of how the message was perceived. At the end of the day, I just wanted love and reassurance. My need for it caused a lot of self-inflicted pain because I was willing to accept red flags in exchange for love and attention. Could you blame me though? Love is a beautiful thing to experience but it can also be dangerous. I grew up around it but I was also shown what love isn't supposed to look like.

I used the memories of my childhood to shape the vision of love I wanted to find. I knew that love was supposed to feel good. I knew that whoever I chose was supposed to love me wholeheartedly and accept me for me. I knew that whoever I chose would have my all, but I wasn't prepared to give my all in exchange for disloyalty. My first heartbreak was tough. I was a hopeless romantic, thinking I could find my man and settle down at the age of fifteen. I laugh at myself now, but could you blame me? My parents were living proof that it could happen. They always told me not to rush into things; of course, I had to learn the hard way. In hindsight, I wish I had understood that love needed boundaries. Being attached was one thing, but what happens when you choose to love someone more than you love yourself?

Bad decisions felt like the right thing to do because, in the moment, my flesh was satisfied. However, my young mind had no idea how much these decisions would impact my future. At this point, what did I even want my future to look like? Getting through college without my weekly check-ins was hard. I realized that grieving didn't look the same for everybody. Sometimes, grief looked like sitting in the corner and crying for hours. Grief will have you randomly laughing at memories as they come to mind. For me, grief also turned into depression for many days.

What is grief exactly? The definition says it's a reaction to loss of someone or something of importance. Depression is a mood disorder that causes a persistent feeling of sadness and loss of interest. It had become hard for me to picture life without the person who helped shape me into the woman I am today. Imagine being in a relationship with somebody going through this. The 18-year-old me didn't understand that the internal battles I was facing couldn't be fought by anyone but myself. I was expecting others to help bring me out of this aura but that led to more unpleasant feelings. I wasn't alone but I felt inadequate. I was convinced that no one would understand me.

Depression has this way of making you feel closed in and I

disconnected from the world completely. I prayed many days for strength and the will to keep going. What my heart wanted most was unconditional love. I knew that I wasn't with my person, but that person loved me enough to give me the greatest gift my soul needed. Nobody knew about our planned pregnancy. I guess you can say I repeated my parents cycle, but for different reasons.

Becoming a mother changed my life and brought me out of a space I didn't think I could escape. From the moment I knew a baby was growing inside of me, my goals were to love, teach, and provide stability for my child. Growing up and meeting people who were raised in household environments unlike mine, made me realize why stability was so important in a child's life. I can count with more than one hand how many times we moved and I had to change schools throughout my childhood. Granted, we moved often because my parents were seeking better opportunities for work. However, the younger version of myself hoped that we could find a permanent place to call home. I didn't enjoy making new friends and then leaving them to start over in a new place. By the time my parents purchased their first home, my ability to adapt in most situations was superior.

Growing up with my parents made me mature faster than most kids my age. As a young teen, I desired attention and sought validation from boys whom my dad told me to stay away from. My desire to love and be loved made me blind enough to do and accept things I shouldn't have. I was supposed to love myself enough to walk away from situations that were clear red flags. Why didn't I? The truth is I didn't want to be alone. The younger version of me was so focused on having someone in my presence that I didn't realize my presence was the gift. This didn't resonate with me until after I gave birth to my daughter. Any mess that I had accepted before would no longer be tolerated because I had to lead by example now. Enough was enough. When the last red flag was thrown, I accepted my new role as a single mother. I knew it would be challenging but my experiences as a child helped shape the vision of the parent I sought to be. Meanwhile, the hopeless romantic in me still hoped that "my person" would come find me and make everything in our lives better.

Did he find us? Yes! But God sure does have a funny sense of humor. During my single season, I learned a lot about myself. I was able to tap in and discover the things that made me whole. I became less dependent and appreciated time with myself. This version of me understood that I didn't need anyone to validate me. I didn't need to call anyone over for something to do when I had nothing to do. I was focused on raising my daughter and becoming a better version of myself. Being a single mother weighed on my mental health some days. It was when I needed people the most that made me realize giving myself to men (who didn't value me or check in on my mental state) was a waste of time. I could no longer give myself to those who would not reciprocate my energy.

During a talk with God, I promised to save myself for marriage, in hopes to keep my spirit grounded and to date with intent. To my surprise, the person I needed had been with me all along. When you put someone in the friend zone, you don't really consider taking them out. I was always told that best friends form the best relationships. After contemplating what I really wanted, everything became so clear. How could a foundation, built from love and authenticity, crumble? I already knew I had someone in my corner who recognized my value, encouraged me to be great, and expected nothing in return. Contributing peace to my mental state made me want to do anything and everything for this man. He deserved it. We deserved each other but soon found out love wouldn't be the only thing we needed to keep us together. Most marriages fail after the first year. Our lives changed so fast. I went from having one child to three. We became home owners and, soon after, added another addition to our family. From the outside looking in, everything was great, but if I could give any advice about things to do before marriage, it would be to go to therapy. Sometimes, a third-party is necessary when you can't seem to understand the other person's perspective. It's easy to say that communication is key, but communication is more than just words. A conversation is carried by tone and that tone can determine whether the conversation is productive or not. Let's just say that before we made it into a therapist's office, my husband and I had a lot of unproductive conversations. We would talk ourselves into circles, both saying valid points, but not listening to understand one another. We wanted the same things but found it hard to function pouring out of empty cups. I felt like I was losing myself and my best friend. Someone who was always so sweet to me suddenly became short and distant. At least that's how I perceived it. My man was really tired and overworked. I was so focused on my needs and wants that I neglected to show my appreciation for him and the things he was doing for our family.

Therapy helped us understand why we were unaligned and allowed us to explore how the experiences from our childhood still affected how we responded to situations and viewed love. Prior to therapy, I hadn't considered the importance of discussing childhood trauma and triggers between each other. I honestly didn't know I had triggers until we were mid-argument one day and I just broke down crying. I never wanted to raise my children in a household that felt unsafe. Although I knew my husband would never hurt me, the toxicity of arguing made me think back to the times where I would sit in the corner of my room, as a kid, and cry because I could hear my parents fighting in the other room. At this moment, I knew life had to change. I knew that it was time for me to own my truth and accept myself for who I was now. I could no longer be that scared little girl allowing my past to affect how I responded to present situations. I had to let that hurt go. It wasn't fair to anyone, especially me. Depression made it easy for me to blame myself and question my role in our lives. Sitting in therapy made me realize that life could be so much better if I just made it that way. We discussed the law of attraction and how to obtain the things we wanted by simply creating the space for positive opportunities. If I want a healthy marriage, I will have a healthy marriage because I will do the work needed to make sure my spouse feels safe. After going through this process, I knew that I had made the right decision. Being vulnerable and having these hard conversations showed me all I needed to know about my marriage. Watching my partner step out of his comfort zone, and actively work towards being a better man, made me feel like we could get through anything life had to offer.

One could define destiny as a predetermined course of events, often held to be an irresistible power of agency. I may not have understood during the struggle, but now I understand why these things had to happen. My trials and tribulations helped me grow. I was able to find my purpose in the midst of adversity and conquer every obstacle thrown my way. I don't have to question my worth or wonder if I'm enough. I understand my value as a woman. I value my purpose as a wife and mother. I have grown and know how to take accountability. I'm not ashamed of my past. Instead, I embrace the future and admire my growth.

Self-discovery can be so enlightening. The journey never stops. Over time, we evolve; but it's the ground work we put in that sets the tone for achieving greatness. After years of making excuses for myself, I've vowed to stop and make progress instead. Awareness is the knowledge or perception of a situation or fact.

How often have you been wrong because your perception wasn't clear?

Are we giving ourselves grace during these times of uncertainty?

Are we communicating with our loved ones so they understand how to help or communicate with us as we heal?

These are all things to consider as we go through our journey. Reflecting back, I actually got everything I manifested and more. I kept God close and He answered my prayers. I could never blame anyone for how my life transpired because I didn't always make the right decisions. I live with no regrets. I only make room for love and affirmations.

I'm not damaged.

I am beautiful, assertive, wise, determined, youthful, and aware!

About the Author – So'leil Thompson

Meet So'leil Thompson is a God-fearing wife, mom, authoress, and entrepreneur from Hoffman, NC. Through her journey of self-discovery, she has found purpose in motivating others through her brand that promotes self-love, mental wellness, and body confidence. For more information and to discover all the ways you can connect with her, visit: **linktr.ee/bawdyxleil**

CHAPTER 2 - JAKIA JONES

Girl, Get Somewhere and Sit Down!

It was many years ago when I was awakened at some crazy hour of the early morning, I don't know, maybe around 3 or 4am. I was sharing the bed with my then boyfriend and father of my child. I looked over at him and he was still in a deep sleep. "Could this be You talking to me, Lord? I'm deep in my sin, lying next to a man I am not married to, and You mean there is something You want to say to me? Right now?"

I always believed in God because, like most people where I am from, my family raised me to be a believer in Christ. The one thing I remember about my childhood is that my mom taught me to pray and that it was part of my bedtime routine. However, when I look back, I don't really remember my parents going to church or taking me to church. Somehow, I had Christ in my heart, and I knew him. When I was about 9 years old, we moved from NY to NC and I remember my grandfather taking me to an old country church at the end of a dirt road. I remember crying because I was scared to see people shout and dance in the holy spirit. I guess at that age, you don't really understand what is happening and it can look like something is hurting the person because they often would scream and cry like they were in pain.

I remember because that little country church at the end of that dirt road was the place I learned that God holds you accountable for your sins. I was afraid and felt guilt and shame each time I did something I knew was not pleasing to God. I had gotten saved in that little church by the age of 12, but I was still not really sure of exactly who God was. I just knew I was a bit afraid of Him and didn't want to make Him mad.

As you can probably tell, by just reading the bit I have revealed, I thought of God as the task master and the one who is full of wrath and wouldn't let people have any fun or He will punish you. Honestly, this is the experience of many, and this is the very reason they walk away from the church and stay in their sin. One might believe it is impossible to live a life pleasing to God and choose to just live and deal with the consequences in what they believe the afterlife to be. I was taught that if you sin you are going to hell, and if you do what is right you will go to heaven.

Every Sunday, someone in that little country church would get up and testify that the Lord would be returning soon and that we needed to get ready. It would scare me so much that I would repent over and over again so I would not be left behind when the rapture comes.

I guess once I became a teenager, and I could no longer be convinced so easily that Jesus was about to come back so I began to take some risks. I lost my virginity at the age of fifteen. I knew what I had done was wrong and I wrestled with the guilt of it every time I committed the act, but it still wasn't enough to make me stop. I dated and married the person I lost my virginity to and thought to myself, "Well Lord, he was the only one and I've married him so surely You have forgiven me for all the years of fornication I did before the wedding."

I lived a pretty religious life after the wedding. I didn't drink, I didn't smoke, I didn't use profanity, I went to church and bible study, I was a good wife, daughter, sister and friend. I always went out of my way to help people. I was convinced that my life was pleasing to God because there was little to no identifiable sin. The problem was I didn't feel like myself. I felt like I had to be this person because if I didn't then God would not be pleased. In my younger days, I liked to sing and dance to secular music. I enjoyed being with my girlfriends. I liked to participate and lead group activities. I was overall more social. As a married woman, I was none of those things. I did nothing

17

of the sort and my life was what I felt to be kind of boring.

Here is where things get good! My husband and I divorced after about 10 years together and 4 of those years married due to some scandalous reasons, but I'll save that for another time. One would think divorce would be devastating after living a picture perfect life for over a decade. Well, the truth is that divorce was my ticket out of my boring life. A reason to be angry with God so I could sin and not feel guilty. After all, I did what was right and the divorce was not my fault so that's a free pass, right Jesus? I was relieved that I got out of the marriage and could get an opportunity to explore who I was outside of being this person I felt I had to be.

I quickly found my language getting more and more vulgar, my clothes getting more and more revealing, my surroundings more and more dark and dangerous, my friend circle larger and more diverse, my drinking more and more frequent, and my number of sexual partners increasing. It's kind of strange because I was becoming unrecognizable, even to myself. Yes, I had a blast, but every day I had to push that little voice to the back of my mind saying, "You are out of the will of God." Honestly, I was having so much fun and felt so free at the time that I didn't want to hear it.

From church every Sunday and Wednesday to hanging out every night and partying in the club on the weekends, how in the world did I get here? You are probably thinking I am going to tell you how I turned my life around and came back to Christ one night in the club or how I had some huge epiphany mid-drink with my girlfriends. Absolutely not! What I am going to tell you is how I went from living what I believed to be a holy life to living like a heathen and enjoying the ride!

Let's just say I've had my share of ups and downs in my life, so there was no way that I was passing up the opportunity to do everything wrong I ever kept myself from doing because of God. In my mind, being good didn't pay off for me and God owed me this time to mess up.

One night after leaving a party and plenty of drinking and dancing, I checked my social media for messages as I normally do. I got a message from a guy I used to go to school with when I was younger. We talked and really had a good conversation and ended up talking until daylight. At the time, I was only looking for fun. I enjoyed the feeling of blowing with the wind and not having to answer to anyone. Especially not God. When I recalled telling my friends about the conversation I had and who I was talking to on the phone, I began to get lots of input about the guy being not the right person for me. I was glad because that is exactly what I wanted, Mr. Wrong and Mr. Right Now. Everyone warned me against getting tangled up with this guy but I had no intentions on listening.

We would make trips to see each other long distance and he lived a wild life and I was all for it. Long wild nights of partying, hot heavy sex, lots of drinking, and just being reckless. I loved it. I loved it so much that when the guy asked me to be exclusive I said yes. I had no idea that God would later use this person to usher me into my destiny.

Well after about a year, the fun came to a screeching halt when I found out I was pregnant. I thought to myself, "I know I can't be pregnant." I was just getting started with my sin! I knew that motherhood was something that was always in me and that I would, without a doubt, make sure my child had a stable and loving upbringing. I knew my time was up and that now I had to sit still and think. I found out I was pregnant about 5 weeks in to my 1st trimester. I was shocked because I thought I couldn't have kids and I was excited because I always wanted to be a mom. I knew I would no longer be partying and living wild. So, for almost 8 months, I sat alone with my thoughts. What a ride!

I had no sex, alcohol, music, or partying to suppress the pain I felt. I had to sit with my emotions and actually process them now. I went into the deepest depression I ever had been in. I watched my whole being change, my life, my body, my outlook on my future. It was really hard to swallow that I had done so much wrong in such a short period of time and even still I was too angry at God to ask Him to forgive me. So, I just stayed in my depression. It became part of my new identity.

Soon the guy from out of town came to live in the city I was in so we could raise the baby together. We decided to take the family life seriously. Our relationship changed and went from fun and free to really serious. We had bills and responsibilities. We both had emotional baggage. We both had issues with trust. It was a really hard adjustment to go from casual dating to full blown family in what seems like overnight. We argued a lot and we struggled and we had so many problems, but something would not let us walk away from the situation.

Years later, I'm still with this guy and our baby is growing healthy and beautiful and things seem to be ok. But it was like every time we tried to get ahead, there was always a setback. I grew weary and began to question if I had made a mistake being with this man. Was this my punishment for being angry at God and doing everything I knew to do that was sinful? Am I sentenced to a lifetime of struggling and confusion? I had grown content and accepted that this was just my life.

One night, I was sleeping and God whispered in my ear, "Seek ye first the kingdom." I knew it was God because I hadn't picked up a bible in years and hadn't prayed or even talked to God in many years. I knew that what I was hearing was a scripture but I didn't know which one nor did I know what the rest of it was. I was afraid because surely God didn't want to talk to me. I'm fornicating, I've had a child out of wedlock, I have pretty much ignored Him. Yet He wakes me up to say something in MY ear? I guess part of me believed that if I pretended not to know God that He wouldn't see all the sin I was doing so when he spoke to me instant shame set in because I knew at that moment he was watching the whole time. Oh my gosh, the things He must have seen, how angry He must be at me.

When I woke up that morning I had talked to my grandmother and told her about the encounter I had had the night before. She finished the scripture for me and told me where to find it in the bible. So of course, I go and grab the bible and find the scripture and I read the entire chapter and I highlighted that scripture. I thought to myself, "God I feel like I sought You before and You left me hanging. What's going to be different this time?" Nevertheless, I was speaking to God again.

According to my google research, to seek has been defined as *an attempt to find, an attempt or desire to obtain or achieve, or to ask for something from someone.* Well, if I'm being honest, I never did any of these things pertaining to God. I just went along with what I was told about God and I lived accordingly. All I knew is I was totally unfulfilled in my understanding of a holy life and was also unfulfilled and not making any progress in my sinful life, there just had to be more.

I started reading the bible more for understanding and I was real with God about things, I presented myself as I was and not what I thought I should be. I felt something happening. I felt a relationship happening. Like I was getting to know someone I had not met before. I did not stop sinning, however. I was still laid up with my boyfriend every night, had a foul mouth and felt like I needed to be in control of everything. I felt things were not changing fast enough for me and I became frustrated with God again. I didn't understand, you said seek you and all this stuff would be added unto me. Well, where is all the stuff God? Now looking back, I imagine God laughing at me because I must have sounded ridiculous.

I was reading, started going to church again, got involved with all these agencies in my field and the money just fell through each time, I was still unhappy in my relationship because I wanted to be the head of the house and that lead to conflict. I almost gave up but God opened my eyes one day and made me understand that I was really just doing too much. I decided I was gonna help His word come to pass. He told me plain as day, "Have you learned nothing from trying to impress me with your works? Get somewhere and sit down and I will tell you what to do, how to do it, and when to do it – but you need to focus on the relationship with me. I am good, I am not who you think I am. I am not who they told you I was, seek Me and find Me for yourself and then I will add unto you."

I'm like, "Ok God, because nothing is working and truth is I'm tired of the same stuff all the time. I just want to feel joy again." Honestly, I didn't know if I could ever feel real joy again, besides when my daughter was born. So soon after that, I committed whole heartedly to my then boyfriend and we were married and he is now my husband. I gave my life back to the Lord after that. After some time, we opened 2 businesses and got great jobs. My husband started going to church with me and my daughter was growing up the way I always wanted as a child, in a peaceful and loving environment. I didn't have to pretend to be someone I wasn't with God or with my husband and it was in Christ that I found my true identity.

God showed me who He was first; not a task master, not the wrathful punisher, but a good Father who loves His children no matter what they do. He is a merciful and forgiving God who never left me, even in my sin. He took His time to come to me in the middle of the night and initiate a conversation that we are still having to this day. He took away the sinful desires I had. He took away the anger, the resentment, the guilt and the shame. He made me understand that it was all in His plan. He orchestrated the encounters and turned all the bad around for my good. No matter how good or how bad I thought I was, I was always chosen to be His and He loves me no matter what. He kept His word. He added those things unto me just because I sat still and let Him worry about all the details. I just sought Him out and got to know Him for who He truly is.

You see, we cannot want what God wants for us if we do not know His heart. When we get to know Him, we become like Him. That is when you begin to see things change. I was looking for something to fill a void and called myself running away from God but ran right into Him. He is everywhere and now I know that He was never gonna let me get too far away. I'm so glad to say that today, I am who I am fully and I have joy and peace. My life is so much better with Jesus as my Savior. I am glad I now know what it really means because I had to seek Him for myself to find out.

About the Author – Jakia Jones

Jakia Marshall Jones is a compassionate mental health and substance abuse therapist, devoted mother, and wife, who draws from her own journey of healing to support others. Having navigated childhood trauma, she understands the profound impact of pain and the transformative power of faith. Through her work, she helps clients find hope and resilience, guiding them to see that Jesus Christ is the ultimate source of healing.

In addition to her therapeutic practice, Jakia is a natural haircare specialist who creates her own line of all-natural products, celebrating authenticity and self-expression. She believes that caring for one's self—both inside and out—can foster deeper connections with God and with others.

With a heart dedicated to serving, Jakia aims to inspire others through her writing, sharing insights on mental health, faith, and personal growth. Her mission is to encourage readers to embrace their journeys, knowing that healing is possible through Christ's love and grace.

CHAPTER 3 – SHERITO SMITH

A Diamond that Found it Rough

She didn't always know she was a diamond. In fact, for most of her life, she felt more like a lump of coal—pressed down, buried under the weight of self-doubt, fear, and the voices of those who said she'd never be enough. The pressure was suffocating, the darkness overwhelming. But what she didn't realize at the time was that much like the diamond, the process she was enduring wasn't meant to break her, but to shape her. The fire wasn't there to destroy her—it was there to refine her.

The making of a diamond is a violent, intense process. Deep in the earth's crust, carbon is subjected to extreme heat and pressure. In the midst of what seems like chaos, transformation is happening. Something common, something that appears insignificant, is being shaped into one of the most precious and unbreakable stones known to man. But the diamond doesn't emerge sparkling and flawless; it first appears rough and unrefined, needing to be cut, shaped, and polished before its brilliance is revealed.

She was no different. For the sake of this story, she was I - Sherito Smith. Life's pressures had attempted to bury my potential. The weight of low self-esteem, the whispers of self-sabotage, and the unrelenting grip of fear kept me hidden. I didn't yet understand that my trials were designed to transform me into the woman God had always seen me to be. I was a diamond in the making—a diamond that found it rough.

It was in the rough where I would discover my strength. It was in the darkness that I would learn to listen for God's voice. And it was through the fire that I would emerge—refined, unbreakable, and ready to walk into my God-ordained purpose.

This is the story of a woman who found herself in the struggle and allowed God's refining process to bring out the brilliance that was always within. A woman who learned to trust the voice of her Creator above the voices of her critics. A woman who became a diamond.

I often kept my head down, avoiding the gaze of others. For years, this had been my comfort zone—hiding. Hiding from the call of God, hiding from the purpose that was etched into my spirit long before I was born. The whispers of doubt, the crushing weight of fear, and the relentless grip of self-sabotage had been my constant companions. But why?

Could it be because of my mother? Other family members? My surroundings? People in ministry? Failed relationships? Internal conversations?

Don't be shocked. If you could be honest, this has probably been your story as well. And people have the nerve to say, "I can't believe that was your life." They forget that we all come from something and someone.

I was a runner. A proverbial track star if you will. I was NOT trying to do this "ministry" thing and I had no desire to have a title. By the time I got into the church, I was just trying to serve. Pray? Teach? Nah, not me. I just wanted to make sure that my late spiritual mother, Apostle Diane Brooks, was good. Ironically, saw me from day one and refused to let me settle. One thing about her, she was not into the excuses or games. She spoke life into me while pulling me into a place of obedience by washing me with the Word of God.

But I can't even lie. I fought it. I fought tooth and nail.

How do you fight to become who God says you are when

you're always being told who you're not? That was my reality and that was just one of the things I had to overcome, in order to step into - you guessed it - a moment of fulfilled alignment and obedience.

I had to accept the call on my life. The call to ministry. And God sent confirmation after confirmation after confirmation to me - back to back. I went through phases, yes. But I ultimately had to answer to the title and the towel associated with the *Apostle.*

In this day and age, there are many opinions about women in ministry - let alone female apostles. If I were to listen to the whispers and naysayers, I would not be walking in the favor and access that God had for me all along.

If you leave it to the world, they'll condemn you for saying *yes* to God. Between traditional church doctrine and the demons of denominations, scriptures are and have been misconstrued for centuries. In these environments, women who feel called to apostolic ministry often face opposition or are told that their calling is either misunderstood or misplaced. Naturally, these views can create significant internal conflict for a woman, making her question whether her calling is truly from God or just a personal ambition.

But let me stop you right there. Being an Apostle was *not* my ambition. Of all the things I could have been, that was not on my radar. Did I understand that it was who I was to become? Eventually, yes. But did I want it? Nope! Not at all. Truth is that anyone who is sincerely called and chosen to be and do anything great for God really doesn't "want" that title.

I wanted to be obedient, yes. I wanted to please God, yes. I did not, however, believe that the title was necessary in order for me to function. I'm low-key and I serve. I serve from a pure place, I serve where help is needed, and I serve how God instructs me to. But this time, I couldn't serve from the back. I couldn't serve behind anyone else. I had to step out. And many years ago, my late spiritual mother told me that this would be my portion. This was probably the one time I wished that she weren't an accurate prophetic voice in my life.

In my younger years, I remember questioning everything about me. I didn't like how dark my skin was, I didn't like my shape, I didn't like how certain body parts looked. I was made to feel that I wasn't valuable; therefore, I sucked at valuing myself. From people in my own home to "friends" and guys I dated - I always seemed to be an afterthought. A second choice. Therefore, I had to learn to protect myself from that standpoint. I would hurt others before I allowed them to hurt me.

I had no idea that God was pouring His Spirit on me and in me, even when others couldn't see me. I learned later in life that scriptures like Joel 2:28-29 were directed to even dark little girls like me. The NLT version says, "I will pour out my Spirit upon all people. Your sons and daughters will prophesy." But had I been given that scripture as a teenager, I would have laughed in your face because *who*?!

Growing up without feeling pure love from my parents, especially with unresolved mommy and daddy issues, created some deep fears that I carried for years. These fears were a constant presence in my mind, shaping how I saw myself and how I interacted with the world around me.

I spent so much time worrying that I wasn't wanted. It felt like no matter what I did, I would never be enough, and that fear stuck with me. I constantly wondered if other people, even friends, would leave me, just like I felt emotionally abandoned at home. The fear of being rejected made me anxious in relationships—I always had this nagging feeling that at any moment, someone would decide they didn't want me anymore.

It felt like I was invisible. I grew up thinking something must be wrong with me because if my own parents couldn't love me the way I needed, who would? This fear made me question my worth. I tried so hard to be perfect, thinking that maybe if I were "better," someone would finally love me. Deep down, though, I was scared that no matter what I did, it wouldn't change how people felt about me.

I always felt like I wasn't good enough. It didn't matter what I achieved or how hard I tried, there was this voice inside telling me that I'd never measure up. I doubted myself constantly and compared myself to others, always thinking they were better, more worthy, or more capable. This fear of never being "enough" paralyzed me from pursuing my dreams.

I learned to build walls. The idea of opening up to someone felt dangerous because, in my mind, being vulnerable only led to hurt. I believed that if I let people see the real me, they'd reject me or, worse, use my weaknesses against me. So, I kept people at a distance, even when I desperately wanted to let them in.

I found it hard to trust people. It didn't matter if it was a romantic relationship or a friendship—I was always suspicious of people's motives. I questioned whether they really cared about me or if they were just going to abandon me like I felt my parents had. It made me defensive and sometimes led me to push people away before they even had a chance to get close.

All of these fears and thoughts shaped who I became. They made it hard for me to see my own worth and believe in my own potential. I felt like I was constantly fighting a battle between the person I wanted to be and the person I believed I was—a girl who wasn't good enough, who wasn't worthy of love, and who would always be left behind.

But here's what I've come to learn: those fears and beliefs were lies. They were born out of the wounds I carried from not experiencing pure love as a child, but they didn't define me. It took time, counseling, and, most importantly, a deeper relationship with God to begin healing those wounds. I had to learn how to love myself, how to trust God's love for me, and how to let go of the fear that I would never be enough.

I didn't know then that I was a diamond and I was merely going through a necessary process. Be reminded that diamonds don't just show up shiny. They start as dark coal, unattractive and undesirable. Yet people appreciate them once they've endured their process. Hmmmmm, ain't that funny?

I think that now is the perfect time to recite the lyrics of Mike Jones: *Back then, they didn't want me.....* I'll spare you the remainder. Lol. But I am so glad that I have become and am still becoming the woman I was meant to be. A woman who is worthy of love, success, and happiness. A woman who no longer lets fear dictate her life. It's all because of God.

All of this internal drama and trauma also caused me to almost miss out on love. Real love. Truth is that when a man came along to tell me how amazing I was, I was trying to figure out what he really wanted...because it had to be a trick, right? Right? Wrong!

It is so important to trust God's Voice and the voice of His Prophets. In the face of opposition, doubt, and fear, the most crucial aspect of stepping into one's process and assignment is the ability to trust God's voice above all others. The noise of naysayers—whether they come from inside or outside the church—must be drowned out by the steady, consistent voice of God.

John 10:27 (NLT) says, "My sheep listen to my voice; I know them, and they follow me." A woman called to do anything great for God, called to be a diamond, must trust that if God has called her, He will equip her, protect her, and guide her. It is God's voice that brings clarity and courage in the face of doubt. His voice is always louder than the opinions of people when it is given priority in our hearts.

The role of prophetic voices is also vital. In times of uncertainty, God often uses His prophets to speak life, encouragement, and direction. I can't count how many times I've sat in church as a stranger and ultimately got called out by God. Just as the prophet Samuel anointed David, confirming his destiny as king, prophets are crucial in affirming men and women who are called to lead.

I could go on and on about the vitality of the right voice and the right mentorship. But I have to stop and remind you that every negative thing that happened to me *had to* happen to me. And it's because destiny called for me. God called for me.

The world offers mixed and conflicting messages, but it is the voice of God that must guide our steps. Trusting His voice—and the voices of those He sends as prophets—enables us to break free from fear, doubt, and societal expectations. It empowers us to step into our calling with boldness, knowing that if God has ordained us then no one can stop us.

As Romans 8:31 (NLT) so powerfully declares, "If God is for us, who can ever be against us?" Again, I say, "Who?!?" The answer is NOBODY - not even ourselves.

I was a Black woman—a daughter of the Most High God— yet the chains of low self-esteem shackled me from fully embracing the power that flowed within me.

But one day, the voice of God reminded me that I was chosen. It reminded me that the Spirit of the Lord was and is upon me. It reminded me that there was an undeniable authority within me. And no, I could not continue in silence, disobedience, and doubt.

God was calling me out. He was calling me out of that hidden place to a higher place. He was pulling on the woman who was healed to go and heal. He was pulling on the woman who had been taught to go and teach. He was pulling on the woman who had been delivered to go and deliver.

Self-sabotage and low self-esteem could no longer be my silent killers. I had to show up boldly and kill them before they could kill me.

The thing about self-sabotage is that it is sneaky. It cloaks itself as wisdom, caution, or practicality, when in reality, it's fear in disguise. Fear isn't just an emotion; it is a spirit—one sent to cripple and stop you from walking into your God-given purpose. 2 Timothy 1:7 (NLT) says, "For God has not given us a spirit of fear and timidity, but of power, love, and self-discipline."

Low self-esteem was the cousin to self-sabotage, always there to confirm the lies. Where fear said, "You can't," low self-esteem said, "You never will." When those 2 got together, they would cover up the diamond and only put forth the coal.

Abuse made me compromise. Silence made me bitter. Disobedience made me uncomfortable. But I heard a word. And over time, that word took root. That seed took root. And in June of 2023, what once was became what had to be.

I stopped running.
I finally found it - even if it was rough.
I decided to stand up and receive what God had for me all along.

Yes I was already in ministry. But even I was comfortable where I was. I didn't want anything that looked like elevation, especially in front of others.

Isn't it funny how we try to hide when we're really in plain sight?

For a moment, I wrestled, but something stronger was pulling me up higher. I made a decision to no longer be silenced by fear. God was calling me into the fullness of my purpose, and weapons were not given permission to prosper.

In this moment, I'm reminded of Jeremiah 29:11 (MSG) and I want to wash you with that Word: "I know what I'm doing. I have it all planned out—plans to take care of you, not abandon you, plans to give you the future you hope for."

I need you to believe it. Why? Because there is a diamond in you.

The moment you can hear and believe the voice of God, there is no going back. His voice is always louder. His voice is always clearer.

There will always be naysayers. There will still be people who doubt you, who question your decisions, who whisper behind your back. But now, your response must be different. You're merely a diamond, going through the process, who found it rough.

My journey wasn't easy, and it wasn't without challenges. But each time that fear tried to creep back in, I remembered that God had already spoken over my life. Every step forward was a step in obedience, a step of faith. And each time I wanted to quit, the words of Isaiah 41:10 (NLT) steadied me: "Don't be afraid, for I am with you. Don't be discouraged, for I am your God. I will strengthen you and help you. I will hold you up with my victorious right hand."

If you're reading this, perhaps you see a bit of yourself in my story. Perhaps you, too, have been battling self-sabotage, low self-esteem, or fear. But let me tell you this: God has already spoken over your life. His plans for you are good, and He has equipped you for everything He has called you to. Diamonds are forged under pressure so everything that you have been through will work for your good. Trust His voice and His process. Silence the noise of the naysayers, the doubters, and even your own fear.

God's voice is the only one that matters. He's calling you to step out, to rise up, to walk boldly into your purpose. You don't have to be perfect; you just have to be willing. Will you stand up today? Will you say yes to the God who has already gone before you? Will you receive the gift of becoming the diamond? Or will you hide and try to do it your own way?

Remember, it's not by your strength, but by His. As you step out of this rough place, know that God's got you. Fear may knock, but faith answers. So be the diamond who walks in faith. You have to because someone is depending on you.

I was the diamond who found it rough. And now, I am encouraging you to recognize that there's diamond in your DNA. God says so and that's that!

About the Author – Sherito Smith

A Maryland native, turned NC resident, Apostle Sherito Smith submitted her life to God on March 8, 1999. Not long after, she began serving under the tutelage of the late Apostle Diane S. Brooks of Rhema Life Word Center (RLWC) in Salisbury, MD. During her time at RLWC, she served at various levels of ministry, including Deacon, Minister, and Elder. She also worked ministry via the

Usher Board, Pastoral Care, and Finance Committee. Pastor Smith was the Office Administrator for RLWC and served as the Armor Bearer to Apostle Brooks from 2000 until her transition on January 2, 2020.

Extensive training and study were completed, ranging from spiritual warfare and deliverance to business operations of the church. In 2013, she, alongside her husband (Apostle Les Smith), and 2 of their 4 children, moved to Sanford, NC. In 2016, Answer The Call Ministries was established. It was at Answer The Call Ministries that she was ordained Pastor on February 8, 2018, and later affirmed as Apostle in June 2023. She graduated from Mt. Carmel School of the Prophets, under the teaching of Apostle Anthony & Prophet Ruth Flowers, on August 28, 2020. With the God-led coaching mid-wife, Apostle Shawna Lathan, she birthed the prophetic in August 2021.

With 24 years in healthcare administration, she currently serves as Practice Manager III for Virtual Care Services Primary Care at UNCPN. She has also served as President of the Administrative Professionals Conference Committee, taught Diversity & Inclusion classes, and contributed to planning the new Surgical Tower.

In December 2022, she released her first book, entitled, "I DO! STILL, I DO!: A 15-Day Devotional Journal for Wives & Wives to Be." She continues to co-labor in ministry with her husband, Apostle Les Smith, at Answer

The Call Ministries in Sanford, NC. To some, she is known as a counselor; to others, she has been a source of God's light. But anyone who encounters her passion and wisdom will recognize that she is sincere about Kingdom business and desires that all aspects of our lives align with the Word of God - not just church. She teaches, encourages, and models life based on the philosophy, "God and God alone!"

SHERITO SMITH

CHAPTER 4 – IBADAN MACK

After the Flash

How did I get here? "Nigga," she called me. "Bum with a job," is what she said. No longer "her" man was the declaration from the woman sharing my last name. Waking up to an empty closet, trash bags stuffed with most of my clothes, and an upset stomach was the start to my summer of 2017. With vain threats of being evicted by the police, I was forced to evacuate the only home I had just to return to the one place I never wanted to see again - my father's house.

As I drove down the road attempting to recover from the verbal assaults that came at the hands of the woman I vowed to spend the rest of my life with, and how the level of vitriol had left me in a state of dismay and disbelief, all I could hear in my spirit was music. The song by William Murphy that proclaimed everything was working for my good resounded. And just like Anthony Brown & Group Therapy sang, I had to trust in God and believe that "this" was leading me to a better place. But how could I believe that at this point? "God, this is marriage number three!"

Was I perfect? No. Was she perfect? No. But God, I tried to do everything a husband was supposed to do and still I find myself here...at the end of another separation and pending divorce. Another relationship that has gone to hell in a handbasket. It seems that everything in my life that I've touched has crumbled and fallen apart. At this point, I was out of options. Nowhere to run, nowhere to turn. My rock had hit bottom and my life was officially in a place of uncertainty. I had been cast out and dismissed by the person I vowed to love in such a vicious and vile way, that I had to pretend it didn't happen by embracing a fantasy of relief to delay the onslaught of pain and remorse. Still, I knew I would eventually have to unpack, review, and learn from this moment once again.

My family and I had been estranged for some time; but in my moment of desperation, they were what kept me from being homeless. The day of reckoning had arrived. I couldn't run from my past any longer. I had to go home. I had to face whatever was waiting for me. I was now headed to a place I hadn't been in many years. A place that contained scars, regret, secrets, and unanswered questions. Home. Yet here lied the death of who I was, my deliverance, personal resurrection, and rebirth. My road to Damascus was just beginning. As I began my walk for me to understand my present circumstances, God had to lead me through my past. Something I spent much of my life locked away in an imaginary closet in my mind avoiding. It was time to step out and discover who I was. To understand who I was, I had to understand the roots of dysfunction that had conceived me, which was my family. I grew up in a household where civil war was a daily occurrence.

On one side, you had my mother and myself; on the other, when he was home, was my father and sister. My father has run from, and still to this day runs from, anything that resembles challenge and responsibility. Someone should have told him that my mother came rolled up into those times one hundred. With them, you had two people from a two stoplight town in Bishopville, SC who made the decision to run away together and get married. However, they didn't take the time to do the proper dating interviews before marriage. Enter saying, "I do." Insert marrying a stranger.

Mix the two and what comes out is a myriad of issues that continue to manifest over the years. Those years included a child born out of infidelity, which was hidden from me for years. My sister and I were born into a war zone and became caught in the crossfire. I grew up a skinny, frail kid who was and still is hated by his older sister for being born and rejected by his father because he never had a relationship with his own father. My mother looked for the husband she always wanted and the father she never had in my father. When her dysfunctional tendencies brought out the "Ahab" in him, he took a job where he managed and would help fix the bottom line of retail stores up and down the east coast. All the while, he was neglecting his own house. His neglect led my mother to a place of deep seated resentment which grew into years of physical and verbal abuse. Because I was the male heir, I was the one who paid for the sins of my father. Room not clean. A** whooping with the biggest switch she could find. Misspelling of my name either written or spoken. A** whooping with a belt until my skin was broken and bleeding. Won't eat your brussels sprouts? A** whooping with an electrical cord and sent to bed. Many days I went to school with jeans to hide the bruises. For the first several years, many calls and reports in my bookbag (that were hidden) went home because of behavioral issues that were linked to the wars fought at home.

When my father came home, I would beg and plead with him to stay home, but my requests fell on deaf ears. He knew who and what he married and his peaceful and separate lifestyle was more valuable than protecting us from the assailant that he was partly responsible for creating. So, here I was, starting over again at 40 years old. Broken, embarrassed, betrayed, living out of laundry hampers and trash bags. Assigned to a couch and a living room, feeling like a refugee from another country. While I was grateful for a roof over my head, I was disappointed that at the halfway point of my life, I had nothing to show for it except broken promises and about two weeks' worth of clothing. "God? How did things turn so quickly?"

As I began my walk, the first person God led me to was my mother. At 17 my mother had a major stroke which left her partially handicapped. Before this took place, I overheard my mother have a conversation with my father that cemented everything I suspected concerning him growing up. On this evening in the fall of 1994, my mother went to her bedroom, turned out the lights, and called my father. I was 16 at the time. One thing about my mother, whenever she turned off the lights and sat on the edge of the bed to call someone, it was serious.

I've overheard several of these "serious" calls in the past because I was just a nosey kid. This one was not one I intended to hear. I still believe to this day that my mother leaving the door cracked, which was something she never did, and me walking by and stopping to hear what was said was God's way of preparing me for what was to come. This call was a moment of truth. This was an ultimatum of ultimatums. I remember my mother saying to my father that she was sick of doing it by herself and that she needed him to do whatever he needed to do to be transferred. She also told him that if he didn't do as she asked to not bother coming back at all. In all honesty to me, it didn't matter whether he came back or not. He was rarely there and had little to no input in my upbringing in 16 years. To this day I can't tell you what a father is because I never had one. My mother, over the years due to her own stubbornness and unwillingness to listen to my father or doctors, had gone from type one to type two diabetes and suffered several additional strokes.

Due to her deteriorating health, she could no longer stay at home and required around the clock care. She had moved to several nursing homes and, whenever possible, I would visit. I would sit with her and have conversations; but looking in her eyes, I knew that the woman who was my mother was gone and before me was just a shell, struggling each day to survive. As Thanksgiving 2018 approached and my mother was now in the hospital, it was apparent that my mother's health was continuing to decline. Finally, word came from the doctors that for my mother to survive, she would have to be fed through a tube and depend on a breathing machine for the duration of her life.

My father knew that that was no way for her to live and so did we. I knew that before he decided her fate, I had to make a decision. I had to forgive her. While I despised her for the years of abuse and everything she took from me, I still loved her because she defended me, took care of me, and pushed me to be excellent. She was my mother above all else and without her, I wouldn't have made it to where I am currently. The doctors had her sedated to numb the pain she had been experiencing.

I sat with her for about an hour and looked at her for as much as I could because I knew this would be the last time I would see her. To this day, I don't know whether she heard or understood me. I told her that I forgave her. Her private pain and struggles culminated into traumatic experiences for both me and my siblings. While it wasn't right and inexcusable, it was all she knew and because she did the best she could with what she had, I can find no fault in that.

I love and miss you mom. Time to move on to the next door, which behind it were my father and sister. When I arrived back home, my sister persuaded me to join her church. At the time, it was being shepherded by a man I had known since I was a teen. While I desired to grow closer to God and knew that He was the key to walking everything out that was in front of me, the place of worship that I chose was mired in uncertainty and scandal from the moment I stepped in the door. For starters, the pastor had an issue with me. It'd been like that since I was a teen. He assumed I had one with him, as we came from opposite sides of the tracks.

While he grew up in poverty without a father, he assumed that I had a good middle class life with two loving parents and not a care in the world. This is what occurs when assumptions turn into jealousy which turn into deep-seated resentment. This, of course, clouds the vision of a shepherd. So, for two and a half years while struggling with my own issues of lust, I listened to this hypocrite preach Sunday after Sunday, using my personal struggles shared with him in confidence and those of others in the congregation, as pulpit topics. All while hiding the double life he was leading behind the scenes, which led to his downfall. I've met more morticians than men and women of God and more death dealers than people who want to lead others to deliverance.

I now understand why people would rather watch online than stand in line to go into any sanctuary. The very people who are supposed to be the symbol of holiness are unholy and now many feel unwelcome due to the no judgment zone being a place reserved for the self-righteous. The assembly has been forsaken because the saints no longer resemble saints. As I walked this road, where I expected a helping hand, I found a shovel. Many found me to be damaged beyond repair and a modern day leper.

On top of this, I had a back room accuser that was feeding this false shepherd and his wife every bit of ammunition they could regarding my struggles and past misdeeds that I had shared with them in confidence. This was my sister. The one who advocated for me to come home, only to launch her revenge tour for the love and attention she felt she never received from our mother because of me. "The

Favorite." Her array of unwarranted offenses and microaggressions were transformed into snippets hidden within her sermons over the span of two and a half years. What I thought was a joke was no longer funny because I discovered that I was the source material and the target of the snide remarks and gaslighting she launched from the pulpit.

After the passing of my mother, the warm welcoming home that I once knew was now a place of closed doors and separate lives. This place no longer resembled a home. It was now a prison of closed doors with memories left to roam, which haunted me day and night in my dreams. Dreams of a family that I would never have and a mother I would never see smile again. Because of this, old habits returned. And whatever bed or legs were open, that's where you would find me. Whatever eased the pain and stopped the voices.

It was all about comfort at this point. My father had this thing with him where in his life he needed to be needed by a woman and be able to meet her needs. Sadly, he never showed this same passion for the children he helped create. At my mother's wake, his concern wasn't consoling the family and keeping us strong during a difficult season, but "what was he going to do next" or better yet "who was he going to do next." For my father and his dysfunction, there was no time to mourn; it was time to fill the need.

Before we knew it, not even a month after my mother was buried, mysterious phone calls were being made throughout the night. Whispers day in and day out throughout the bedroom. If you stepped in to ask him a question while on the phone, a look of guilt and an instant pause in the conversation would come until you left. It was as if we were living with a senior citizen child. It didn't take long for everyone to figure out that our father had a new love interest. Instantly his behavior and mood changed.

After my mother's passing, he quit his almost six figure job and started working transporting people for cash citing heart problems, which made no sense. You had a mortgage, barely any retirement savings, car payments, and a list of other responsibilities. On top of that, he had purchased a vehicle for me that I was making payments on, and he was hounding me to provide money for it almost daily. Skirt chasing was always something he had a history of doing. Did my father have an exit strategy that he wasn't telling us about?

Oftentimes, the confrontations were contentious and nasty. At the time, my job was temporary, and I was only getting part time hours, which he knew. In typical fashion, as always, he was blaming everyone around him except himself for the decisions he had made. The once gentleman who welcomed me into his home had gone right back to being the cold uncaring bastard that my mother held accountable growing up. Reality was now starting to set in.

One morning while I was asleep on the couch, my father - who was struggling to make ends meet - yelled at me regarding another insurance payment for the car. This time he wanted twice what I normally pay. I had just worked overnight and was exhausted. The kindness and generosity of him was gone and I now felt that I was living in a home with my mortal enemies. Before I lost my temper and did something I regretted, I called the woman who eventually became my wife, who at the time had a duplex she wasn't using and asked her if I could go there to escape the madness I was experiencing.

She agreed and that night, I packed up my belongings and moved. After cleaning up, I laid down and went to sleep only to wake up the next morning to more evil machinations in the form of an extortion email from my father that was written by my sister. Since I chose to leave without saying anything, my father wanted two months of car payments and insurance, or he was going to pick up the car and he wanted the keys to "his" house. After calling a few people and gathering the money which I didn't have, I gathered the money, the keys, told my sister it was all in the mailbox, and drove away. I vowed never again to step foot in my father's house.

All of my life, he showed me I was nothing more than a needless "obligation." When my mother passed, so did his responsibilities. Eventually after a month, my sister set a meeting between my father and herself, using the false shepherd as a mediator. Nothing came of the meeting other than blame being placed squarely on my shoulders for how everything happened, but I expected nothing less from a man who idolized my father and despised me. I only took the meeting in hopes of reconciliation; however, in typical fashion, my father again dropped me like Mephibosheth, leaving me lame in both feet and wondering why fatherhood is something he continually ran from. About a month later, my fears had been realized when my sister revealed to me that my father made the decision to move back home and get married to a woman he dated in high school.

Super save a skirt was now slowly, but surely, transporting his belongings to South Carolina, leaving the sister to figure what to do with a house that she didn't own. My mother, his ex-wife, had not been buried a year before engagement flyers and rings were exchanged. At this point, I just wanted to dress up like the joker and sit on the porch laughing all day because my family couldn't be this f***** up. To make matters worse, on Thanksgiving of that year, I pulled up at work only to get off work and my car was gone. I called the lienholder, who then transfers me to the bankruptcy division.

Now it all makes sense. This is why I haven't seen or heard from him since he hightailed it out of town. He was tying up loose ends to start a new life. Damn telling us! Typical coward. I called him. He wouldn't answer the phone. That was five years ago. I haven't tried to call him since, and he hasn't picked up the phone to call me. Some people will always have an issue facing those they know they have failed. Since then, he's sent party meat, canned goods, cologne, and a picture; but still, no phone call. My sister, whom he also left behind, made the decision to reconcile and position herself to inherit whatever he leaves behind. All the while ignoring his wrongs and neglect when it came to me, because all she's concerned about is herself. As I stood before this door I asked God how I was able to forgive two people who opposed me since birth.

How could I pardon the people who rejected me for attempting to do nothing more than love them? Then He spoke to me. He told me that love and acceptance was something they decided long ago that they were not going to give to me. God had to show me that some people are incapable of giving you love and acceptance because they never received it at any point in their own lives. Like scavengers, they searched the earth looking for it in whatever and whoever they could find, only to come back with empty fulfillment which equated to empty and hollow souls.

Because of this, even though I was still hurt by how I was cast out, I chose to forgive. I closed the door and walked to the next. Finally, I came to the last door. I had to confront the failed relationships and broken hearts I left behind. For over 20 years I porned, fornicated, masturbated, and adulterated my way to divorce several times. This led to a trail of trauma, broken hearts, and promises. For many years I was no good to anyone and couldn't understand why.

Then God spoke to me one day and revealed to me that part of the reason he brought me home was to see the very source of my dysfunction. The entire time, I was living under my father's roof, I was staring my dysfunctional doppelganger in the face. For most of my adult life, everything I did mirrored my father, the relationships. The decision making. The Ahab tendencies. The revelation was mind blowing. The man I knew very little about I was more like than I could have imagined. God further revealed to me that who I became was not my fault. This is why, during my years of dysfunctional living, He spared my life. And now that He had revealed the source, deliverance was up to me.

The rest of the road was not easy. But in confession, I found freedom. In forgiving myself, I found the ability to start over. In seeking to take responsibility for my actions, I sought to reconcile with those I had wronged and to set things right in my own life going forward. Over the years I've had some setbacks, but I remained steadfast and focused to break the generational curses that my mother didn't tell me about. The very ones my father chose not to share. With God's help and never changing hands, I have been able to turn trauma into treasure, as well as cancel every curse so that it will never again consume my life or the lives of my children or any generations to come.

I came to the end of my road and discovered the man that God wanted to introduce me to all along and was able to shed the one dysfunction and generational curses that had draped over God's original design. Now I walk a new path for his glory. Many of us weren't quiet by nature. We'd just been traumatized to the point where we learned to create a closet within our minds and for most of my life that is where I hid. Healing and restoration had to take place in my life, and I pray that this chapter is a testimony to all that wherever you are in life, God still loves you. I know what it's like to continue to lose.

I know what it's like to experience rain with no umbrella in sight. I know what it's like to have people shovel dirt on you because they feel as if you shouldn't be seen. Know that there is victory on the other side of loss. Know that rain that's coming down is preparing you to become a garden that flourishes for God's purpose and that with every mound of dirt you must climb out of, know that the ground that tried to hold you is rich and is fortified because your hands of faith touched each scoop. When I hoped for change, nothing happened. When I envisioned the change, sought the change, and walked as if my situation changed, I then witnessed the manifestation of what my faith will accomplish. Greater is waiting for you on the other side of the flash...

About the Author – Ibadan Mack

Entrepreneur, Trailblazer, Visionary. Ibadan Mack is a native of Fayetteville, NC and is an alumnus of Strayer University & Purdue Global University. Ibadan is a man that strives daily to be an active participant in the up building of his community and empowering everyone he encounters. He believes that people from all walks of life should be empowered and encouraged to be the leaders and pillars of their families and their communities. As a husband and man of faith, he believes in the word of God and its practical application as well as the impact that it has on every faithful man and woman of God. His faith and entrepreneurial spirit have led him to the current development of *We Are Men Clothing Company Inc.* With this new clothing company, which is set to launch in the fall of 2024, his vision is to enact change through various social initiatives and to have a lasting impact that will be seen and felt for generations to come.

CHAPTER 5 – PRISCILLA GEORGE

Healing

I still got joy in the chaos.

Such words sung in rhyme had once left me with a wondrous laugh, for it is hard to imagine someone happy in their darkest times. Swallowed by hardships and enveloped in every lasting issue, I couldn't see through the surface of the lyric.

It was a cold afternoon in the transitional period of fall. When the winds were bringing about change with them. Little did I know that the leaves and the air weren't the only ones that were going to be enveloped in the beauty of conversion.

I was physically at my workplace, but mentally, I was shuffling in my overburdening issues. As a behavioral therapist, it was my responsibility to lend a listening ear to my clients while my overwhelming self was isolated in my mind. I was working with one of my clients that day. And as I kept trying to transition from one activity to another, her denial came upon me like a sign from God.

Priscilla, everything is okay.

That was the last thing I recorded her saying. It felt like God's message dawned upon me through my client. But I, still wrapped up in the storm of everyday life, didn't know the first thing about making things okay.

It felt like the darkness was caving in on me, and loneliness had become my friend. For the light of my life, my father had been sick for years, and the chaos and uncertainty around his health had left me questioning how I would go about my life without his presence. I had called my spiritual Father, Bishop Blessing Samuel, to join me in prayer for the health of my dad.

Healing didn't only seem physical but spiritual, and I dropped down for prayer. Everything seemed to be going into decline; the agony of not finding peace had spiraled me into depression. When the Bishop prayed, he asked me to prepare myself for the acceptance of my dad's purpose on Earth coming to an end.

It had all started to make sense to me at that moment. It already felt like my dad's soul had left Earth to start a life in heaven while his body waited for its departure.

I've built my life on Jesus.
He's never let me down.
He's faithful through every season.

In the changing seasons of autumn, we stand within the unpredictability of winters; Jesus and the Holy Spirit stand firmly, holding onto our bodies to help us survive.

That season was upon me during this period. I vividly remember Father Samuel's words as I let them circle my fogged-up mind while my sisters chatted away. It felt as if I was standing outside of my own body, watching myself go over these puzzles to make the purpose of life evident to me.

I desperately wanted to cling to the *calm before the storm* or the post-storm scenario where some peace could be maintained. Little did I know that signs of peace sparkled through the storm of chaos like seashells traveling in the vast layers of the sea.

The talk about the funds needed for the extraction of mucus out of our dad's mouth for proper breathing jolted me out of my disassociation.

"We won't be needing that anymore..."
My sister's haunting words that revealed the news of my

father's departure sent me deep into thought. A place where I could hear voices singing:

I've still got joy in the chaos.
I've got peace that makes no sense.
And I won't be goin' under
I'm not held by my own strength.
'Cause I've built my life on Jesus
He's never let me down.
He's faithful through every season.
So why would He fail now?
He won't.

It was all God's plan. And I smiled and accepted it wholeheartedly. The loss of my beloved father, a man who loved me dearly, did leave me in tears, but I wasn't going to let it leave my life unanswerable. For I knew that the Holy Spirit had laid a path for me, and I was keen to walk on it, healing every step of the way. This moment, while immersed in the depths of the song, wasn't just a realization. It was a grand epiphany.

An epiphany that sent me into the comforting embrace of the Holy Spirit. His reminder helped me through my struggles to achieve stability and happiness. Intellectual attainment and worldly wisdom are provided to us by the Holy Spirit. So, it is our responsibility to push through and become the people we want to become, free of any issues. Stability is described as such, *a secret and hidden wisdom.*

Stability grounded in peace is a state of mind that carries no explanations. It holds onto the blessings provided by religion. Joy is not simply a fleeting emotion that we experience now and then but remains firm in our hearts, blossoming with hope through the help of the Holy Spirit. The Holy Spirit has given me the strength and the energy to bear all the tragedies in life. Upon hearing the news of my father's death, everybody was surprised at the melancholic peace I was in. I wasn't solely responsible for my courage, but the light of the Holy Spirit bestowed upon me the endurance of pain. He has provided me with ways to dig deep inside my heart to pull out any underlying issues I have been too afraid to confront over the years. To love and to not fear being loved. The Holy Spirit has blessed me immensely in facing fear head-on and dealing with the jumbled thoughts in my mind, arranging them to stabilize my thought process. I was blind in the face of my potential and worth until I realized that we are God-fearing people whose souls have been nurtured in the House of God. So why waste the potential and the love with which He has created us?

The Holy Spirit doesn't simply deliver God's message but also brings a promise to Him—the promise of security and contentment. We just need to reach out to grab it. He is the Spirit of grace and fights against all the demons that plague our minds into turmoil. He is the reason why we exist. Our lives are open to the Word of God. He fights against all hate and helps humans flourish into God-fearing and happy creatures.

The purpose of the Holy Spirit isn't simply to guide us but also to provide us with comfort and peace. It gives us the strength to deal with our overbearing issues. It counsels and comforts us when we need it to do so. The path we have provided us light for is full of hurdles. But we should always remember that those hurdles have solutions as well. The solutions are prayer and the firm belief in God's plan.

"Do not be anxious about anything, but in every situation, by prayer and petition, with thanksgiving, present your requests to God. And the peace of God, which transcends all understanding, will guard your hearts and your minds in Christ Jesus." (Philippians 4:6-7)

The Holy Spirit also guides us through healthy behaviors, good coping mechanisms, and finding an escape from anguish. When our minds are diseased with negative thoughts that we tend to fall victim to, mentally and physically, the Holy Spirit jolts up and rings the bell of belief in our hearts.

"In the same way, the Spirit helps us in our weakness. We do not know what we ought to pray for, but the Spirit himself intercedes for us with groanings too deep for words. And he who searches our hearts knows the mind of the Spirit because the Spirit intercedes for God's people by his will."

(Romans 8:26-27)

My journey started at a random moment when a song paradoxically messaged and provided me with questions answered through the Scripture.

"Rejoice always, pray continually, give thanks in all circumstances; for this is God's will for you in Christ Jesus." (Thessalonians 5:16-18)

My story isn't the only testament to the power of the blessings of the Holy Spirit. A dear friend of mine, who has been blossoming in my life for the past 26 years, had found herself in the darkness of her doctor's message when he told her that she couldn't have a child. The light of the Holy Spirit is so intense that the believers are immediately exposed to the blessings they have long been yearning for. She, miraculously, is a proud mother of two wonderful children. All her agony and sadness withered away as the Holy Spirit revealed God's Plan. The Lord does, in fact, work in mysterious ways.

Similar to her pain was our Bishop, who had been wrongly defamed to the point where rumors about him became the talk of the town. People spread lies about him to assassinate his pure character. His trust in God never moved an inch. It became even more intense as he turned to him in his time of need. And our Lord, who has never turned away from His men, provided him with the kind of peace you find in the same chaos I had found myself in. He left the battle between truth and lies, handing his arms to the Holy Spirit and God's justice to take action. He stood silently, waiting in patience for the victory of goodness to take over. Seeing the pain in his eyes, yet his mouth sealed shut, I found inspiration from his demeanor. It further strengthened me in my beliefs.

These brave souls' attitudes were very contagious. So, as I let these stories consume me, I left the battlefield against lies and evil, for the trust in the courtroom of God had increased within me.

The only thing that you and I have to do is to heal and let the agony wash away. In the void of our daily struggles, depression, and unresolved issues, we should remember that there is a light. A light that shines with the kind of peace we yearn for. And that peace can be found within our struggles. Just like me, everyone deals with problems. But these problems aren't permanently attached to our souls. Rather, they can be easily removed through self-reflection and meditation. God has provided us with lives covered in hurdles, but His plan is not without a cause. God's plan weaves our character development and permanent peace hidden in the apparent darkness. Being a part of this universe for a reason, we must discover the permanence in peace woven in the threads of daily struggles. We are God's creation, and therefore, we are worthy to live magnificent lives with fulfillment.

The Holy Spirit emerges with comfort and guidance as the light of our lives. He symbolizes a path for souls to walk on. When we find ourselves limited or blocked off in the middle of the road, he renavigates and helps us step forth into our journey to discovery. As a guide to becoming more like Jesus Christ, he convicts us of sin and helps us heal from our pain. This healing life-long journey comforts us with the embrace of a Higher Being watching over us and working through our issues along with us.

We are trying to make the best of things when life wounds us, which should be encouraged in everyone's life. Even in the most turbulent of situations, a glimmer of hope in the form of joy can sustain itself. Meditation, breathing exercises, and journaling can be beneficial for helping yourself out. Along with the guidance of the Holy Spirit, clearing out the path for us to land our happiness into, our responsibility is to ensure that we stay on the right path. The Bible recommends renewing our minds and not falling victim to the ill ways of society. The right path is the way to go about life. Staying committed, practicing daily affirmations, taking care of your body, breathing exercises, yoga, and meditation can help us a lot.

To stay mindful isn't just a religiously accepted trait but a psychologically encouraged exercise as well. It transforms our nihilistic views into positive words, our no into yes, and our 'not possible' into 'definitely.'

My past is layered in the tragedy of my identity crisis. I struggled to fit in as a woman who never found her spot in this universe. My insecurities were a magnet to all the wrong people and crowds. With the desire to feel loved and wanted, I let these people envelop the best of me. They would gather the best of me and always took advantage of me. These distractions drifted me away from the purpose God had created for me. The estrangement had come to a point of wanting to end my life. The demonic voices in my head had pushed aside the will of God and made me go astray. Now that I have surrendered my life to Jesus, it has helped me become the best version of myself. I cater to my needs and heal myself throughout. I now know the worth of my existence. I don't settle for anything less than what serves my purpose. This is a lifelong struggle of healing, rinsing yourself of sin, and repeating.

My social circle has now drastically changed, and I now surround myself with people who admire my personality and love me for who I am. As I have mentioned, using words of affirmation helps a lot. I constantly say to myself, *"I'm the prize."* I have a lot of peace in my life now that Jesus is in control of my life, and I can't do anything without the approval of the Holy Spirit. He's not only my Guide, but also a friend I wish the old me had accepted.

Healing should be a part of everyone's life, especially those whose life seems to be stuck in the middle of problems. Our trauma and unresolved hurdles in life collect themselves in our bodies and are manifested in physical ailment. Back pain, heartaches, and indigestion could be a sign of overwhelming trauma collected in the body. It's scientifically proven that our bodies aren't just vessels that collect physical trauma but mental torment as well, showing signs of sickness and body aches. It isn't simply essential for our spiritual essence to be delivered to the One above; our bodies also need closure. Therefore, healing is needed.

But how does one heal oneself? To answer this question, we must look into the depths of the scripture for answers that it unfolds:

"Nevertheless, I will bring health and healing to it; I will heal my people and will let them enjoy abundant peace and security." (Jeremiah 33:6)

The security of receiving our closure is certain from God. Healing is an inevitable part of our spiritual journeys because our Holy Spirit is there to guide the way toward God's blessed healing powers. To heal yourself, you need to realize the potential within you and work accordingly. Healing lies in the realm of the Holy Spirit. Jesus baptized His disciples through the light of the spirit, which is shown in His fellow men, to cradle them against bad health and depression. Jesus brought sight to the blind, revived the dead, and cured the ill, portraying the intensity of the love for God and the Holy Spirit. Being a comforter, the Holy Spirit's healing isn't limited to physical healing but spiritual as well. You find God and realize the power of His love in times of need. Peace in times of chaos. At times, God's sent ailment is like a *thorn in the flesh (2 Corinthians 12:17-10),* but that's where the ability of the holy spirit comes in; it nests the soul in its Divine power and proves how a single thread of belief can weave the healing blanket for the sick.

When the sick, depressed, or mentally challenged people look up to the light of God, Jesus Christ, and the Holy Spirit, miracles make way for them. Never doubt the legitimacy of the healing power of the Divine, for *it works in mysterious ways.* You can get answers through a dream, words on a page of a random book you're reading, or, like me, a song you listen to on a casual afternoon. These epiphanies spiral us into questions that are then answered in the court of the Divine. We need Him, and when we stretch out our arms for help, He comes our way with all the comfort we need.

Let's take the instance of breathing exercises. If we pull out an hour of our day in our busy lives just to sit, without any external interruptions, and let our mind bring peace to us through deep breaths, an effective change can be noticed. Take a deep breath in, becoming one with the universe God has created for us to enjoy, and then let all our anxiety and worry out through an exhale. This is medically proven to be effective; it can provide a spiritual band-aid for all the hollowed-out wounds that have plagued us with worry. Answers will start dawning on you, one revelation after the other. You will become more and more sure of your abilities to conquer the world, and your connection with God, Jess Christ, and the Holy Spirit will be stronger than ever. Hear the sounds of nature, birds calling to the One above, leave rustling in the wind to commemorate a symphony to god and people, running about their day, having a connection with you based on your origin: Our Creator.

Along with breathing exercises, minute and gradual changes can also be effective. Daily exercises like jogging, yoga, running, Zumba, listening to songs that bring peace, etc. It can be effective as well. Expressing yourself creatively, like incorporating hobbies, painting, sketching, and crafting, can develop your relationship with yourself and the power above. We are all sent to this world with a purpose; during our short time, we should try our best to treat our bodies deservingly and prove to everyone, including God, that we are worth the creation. That we have realized the power to heal! To breathe! And to rejoice in hard times. Difficult times are sent upon us like a storm on the sea. As sailors in our boats of life, we need to navigate our way through, for we know and we should assure ourselves that there is calm and peace after the storm. This is a test of how well we can travel in our boat of life and listen to the compass guide, that is, the Holy

Spirit. We need to trust our instincts and work our way through the seas of our destiny to become calmer.

While breathing exercises work tremendously, I tend to meditate on the scripture. Whenever I am having a bad day, I make sure to sing to my Lord as loud as I can to ease my mind. It distracts me from misery while transcending me in a world of angels, God's heaven. A song dawns upon me each time I feel down, and I, knowing that it's a message from God, sing it no matter where I am. The Bible talks about how worship is the assembly of positivity. It is the best kind of meditation you can offer to yourself or others. This has worked for me, along with many people around me, and I am sure that you'll be able to find peace in the chaos of everyday life.

Body workouts like yoga have also been proven to be beneficial. For those who like to work out alongside worship, Yoga doesn't simply include breathing work but also includes exercises that heal the body. Exercise triggers endorphins, which boost our mood, make us feel lighter, and provide a purpose for us to come back to it again. Yoga isn't limited to these benefits but also extends onto our sleep cycle. We get to sleep more peacefully as our bodies relax and get rid of all the collected ailments from trauma. Managing stress and providing closure to our thoughts through yoga is quite helpful.

"For physical training is of some value, but godliness has

value for all things, holding promise for both the present life and the life to come."
(Timothy 4:8)

Exercises and working out have always been encouraged in the Bible. Physical activities in spiritual retreats can remove clutter from the mind and connect us to nature. Our bodies have been sent to us as gifts, and it is our responsibility to take care of these vessels that breathe life into us. Bone strength, cardiovascular strength, and a good immune system contribute to the betterment of our mental health. For our spiritual journeys, ignited by the Holy Spirit, to commence, we need good health. Moderation is also recommended in the Bible. To sustain the good to a limit that it remains beneficial.

Our minds are an ensemble of thoughts. A collection is so vast and overwhelming that sometimes, it's hard for the vessels in our bodies to contain them. That's when distress occurs. The Bible, though it isn't explicit regarding journaling, encourages talking to God in times of need. And what better way to do it than writing it down? Pick a journal that you think might be comforting enough for you to push through your issues and pour your heart out.

I have found journaling to be quite beneficial for my mental health. Growing up, I kept a diary to pour my heart into. I used to pen down my thoughts and feelings. From slight inconvenience to revealing an innocent crush,

I let it all out. Now, as a woman, I use a diary as a ministry book. Whenever I am reading the scripture and a revelation or an epiphany occurs to me, I turn it into prose. Jotting down notes helps me a lot when I'm listening to sermons or topics to preach on. Though, in theory, it seems like a simple act of revealing ourselves to the pages of a book through a pen, it is proven to be very effective. There is depth to it. Self-discovery, navigating our issues, working through them, and figuring ourselves out are some of the many ways of dealing with our problems. There are psychological and spiritual benefits to doing so. Dr. James W. Pennebaker, a well-known writing therapist, believes that,

"Writing can help you connect the dots between your thoughts, feelings, and behaviors."

Imagine our thoughts to be like puzzles. In the box, they are scattered and seem to be too intimidating to reach out to. While some might avoid pulling them out, others who realize the power of compilation will pull each piece out carefully, navigating through and scattering them on the table. The table will become a means for them to see the bigger picture, the pieces will become less threatening, and they will, slowly but surely, work their way through them, gluing one piece to the other and finally be revealed to the masterpiece of a portrait. The portrait is our life, connected by numerous puzzle pieces and hard work, and thorough navigation can take place through journaling.

"Death and life are in the power of the tongue, and those who love it will eat its fruits."
(Proverbs 18:21)

The tongue can, therefore, translate it onto paper. The paper can safeguard our thoughts as we recollect them, reading over them to find resolutions to our problems. Self-awareness is needed to detect our issues and urge ourselves to be better. Journaling also helps with reducing our stress. In our busy lives, we often forget to say a word or two to ourselves, affirming the betterment of our health and happiness. Journaling is a very practical and effective way of fixing issues in our lives. It provides us with a means to connect with God.

Another effective strategy to blossom our relationship with God is through meditation. Different kinds of meditations can be incorporated into our lives to connect our souls to God.

- **Mindfulness Meditation:** is the kind of meditation secluded from the present state of our souls. Living in the moment and focusing on our breathing accordingly helps us concentrate more and push the best out of ourselves.

- **Mantra Meditation:** this is spiritual. It revolves around repeating phrases or words for spiritual affirmation. Chanting it out loud or making it a focal point in your mind helps soothe the pain that has been building in us. It helps with your attention span and breaks short cycles of losing focus. The ability to ease overthinking is practiced through Mantra meditation. Closing our eyes and repeating an affirmative phrase can help calm our minds. In our mind's chaotic abyss, one phrase can persist and wash out all confusion and turmoil.

- **Movement Meditation:** this meditation also caters to breathing. It connects your mind to your body, unifying it in a positive sphere of ease. Quick movements like dancing to your favorite song, exercising, or skipping can push the barrier between the soul and the body away. It reduces stress and makes us more mindful and aware of ourselves and our surroundings.

- **Focused Attention Meditation:** as the name suggests, creating one through a focal point and beginning to befog our minds from there is a part of this kind of meditation. Usually, it begins with focusing on your breath. Take sharp breaths to activate the senses and become hypersensitive to your surroundings. Focused Attention meditation also relies on a single sound, a drum, or a chime. This kind of meditation brings back your focus to a singular entity and makes you aware of yourself and your surroundings.

These are some of the many kinds of meditative methods that are medically proven to be effective. Spiritually, they guide us through our darkest times and reveal a shining sun sent upon us by the guidance of the Holy Spirit. It isn't simply psychology that offers help to create positive coping mechanisms, but the Bible as well.

"The Lord himself goes before you and will be with you;
he will never leave you nor forsake you. Do not be afraid;
do not be discouraged."
(Deuteronomy 31:8)

He is always here with us, ready to clasp our hands if we fall into the depths of depression. Our challenges are nothing but temporary pieces that are added to our lives. The transformative abilities of the Holy Spirit guide us through our lives.

Small mindful changes, reliance on God, Jesus Christ, the Holy Spirit, and self-reliance are important for a complete switch in life. From the shallow waters of depression to contentment, God is with us through and through. We don't carry burdens alone; the Divine hand helps us and makes everyday life easier and happier. Try your best to bring your life on the right track through the guidance of the Holy Spirit and leave the rest to God. For,

"I did the best I could, and I need to let that be good enough."

About the Author – Priscilla George

Author, Minister, Speaker, Special Educator, and Registered Behavior Therapist.

Priscilla N. George expertly balances career, ministry and family. She is the founder of *Get Up Sister Pick Up Your Heels,* a platform to empower women. She graduated with a Master of Arts in Teaching/Special Education and a Bachelor of Science in Family and Consumer Science with a concentration in Child Development and Family Relations from North Carolina Central University. She wants to reach others by connecting to businesses, ministries and those who are doing things in the community to empower others through the gospel. Priscilla believes that presentation shows a lot about one's character and recognizes that you cannot climb the ladder of success dress in a costume of failure. She is a mother, daughter, sister, and friend.

CHAPTER 6 – TYSHANA MABRY-DIAZ

I Forgive Me!

Hey, you. Are you ready to forgive yourself and come from under the dark blanket of shame, guilt, bitterness, and insecurities - into the bright light of freedom, peace, joy, and love? If you are, then this is for you. When I chose this topic, I had you in mind. *Yes, you!* The one who has decided to pivot because destiny is calling. I am glad you are here; I hope you take away a few life lessons from my personal experiences and testimonials. I am inspired to share with you transparent moments of change that shifted me.

Was there ever a specific time in your life when you made a conscious decision to forgive yourself for the things you have done? Surely, we all have made many mistakes and some bad choices. Have you ever thought to forgive yourself for the people you have hurt, lied to, lied on, judged, or misused? Take a quick moment to think about it. Have you ever thought of doing such a thing? Well, today could be the day you uncuff yourself from your self-prison. Are you ready for a self-reflection moment? It's time for you to walk free, but are you ready to live free? Your release papers are approved. No need for a *Monopoly get-out-of-jail-free* card, I know a man who dropped the charges, and He paid it all in full on the Cross just for you.

Let us get right into it. What does it mean to forgive? The definition of forgiveness is *to stop feeling angry or resentful towards (someone) for an offense, flaw, or mistake.* It is also described as *the action or process of forgiving or being forgiven.* Forgiveness can mean different things to different people. In general, it involves an intentional decision to release anger or resentment. However, the act that offended you or has hurt you in the past might always be with you. But, as you begin to work towards the journey of forgiveness, that load will lift and no longer have a hold on you. I want to challenge you to think for just a moment. When was the last time someone told you that they forgive you? How did you feel? Did you receive it? After all, the same God who has forgiven us and all of our sins also wants us to forgive others when they sin against us.

Matthew 6:14-15
[14]For if ye forgive men their trespasses, your heavenly

Father will also forgive you: [15]but if ye forgive not men their trespasses, neither will your Father forgive your trespasses.

Looking back, I wonder if I genuinely meant the apologies I gave out so freely, especially in middle school. I can recall many times when I would act out and become so mean to my friends, classmates, and adults. I called them foul names, and instigated arguments and fights. They didn't deserve what I was dishing out. They had no idea what I was dealing with internally. Sadly, they became my outlet for the mistreatment I acquired. I believe it was a learned behavior.

Growing up, where tough love was the standard and dysfunction was normal, it was easy talking down to others. It was easy to mistreat them, due to my environment.

Have you ever experienced childhood trauma or pain? If you have, I can take an educated guess that you probably were not the happiest kid. This includes at home, in school, or on the playground. If you are like me, with a painful past, you may have endured many challenges. This especially includes in the areas of relationships and trust. Having trust issues throughout my life has hindered many genuine friendships. I spent a lot of my youth years guarded and angry. I adopted the skill of hiding my pain well. I learned early to be silent. I learned how to mask my feelings and hide my emotions. As a little girl, I could not recall receiving many hugs or kisses. No "I love you" or "I support you" or "Your life matters to me." These are words every child needs to hear to feel loved, supported, and important. Have you ever heard the phrase *"misery loves company?"* I have found that phrase to be true. Now that I am wiser and more mature, I recognize that misery does love company. I understand that much better. Looking back, I had an abundance of friends in my younger years when I was miserable and broken. As an adult, that relationship dynamic has shifted because I'm healed, set free, and living for God. I remember receiving compliments for my bright smile growing up. However, I never felt the love behind it all. It was to the point where when someone said or did nice things for me, I would question their motives. Everyone was a suspect and nobody was safe, at least in my book.

I did not want to trust many people so I kept a small circle. I only had a handful of close friends in elementary and middle school. You could say that I was traumatized as a child, dealing with abandonment and rejection issues. Some of the closest people to me were the ones who abandoned me, rejected me, or abused me.

I was raised in public housing (The PJ's) in NYC with my beloved great aunt. She had four kids of her own then fostered three – myself and my two siblings. She did the best she could with what she had. I loved her dearly; God bless her soul. No matter how much she tried, did, or didn't do, she was not my biological mother. She was not the one I longed to be with and live with. My mother was a sweet soul who loved her children and her family, but drugs and alcohol won the war. As a child, I desired love from my biological parents. They both struggled with various addictions.

I can remember being a young girl and so broken, feeling hopeless, without value. I always felt confident in what I wore on the outside but was empty on the inside. At that time, my outer appearance mattered most. I was raised in an environment where what we wore spoke to our status and value. It may sound crazy or foolish to someone who never had to experience this type of environmental conditioning. You may not have had to wonder or worry about what new outfit and kicks to rock outside. You weren't concerned with what to wear to school, to the block party, to Skate Key, or even on Easter.

My actions before the change were conditioned due to my environment. My actions before the change were because I was conditioned by my environment. I was influenced by a lot of poor communication. Due to my lack of communication, I would lash out. I did not want to feel what I felt, so I avoided hard conversations. I would avoid relationships and avoid getting to know new people. Being scarred from previous relationships or by family members and friends, I found myself not wanting to open up. Being guarded and refusing to open up, with so many barriers and layers of trauma and unforgiveness, hindered a great deal of my growth and relationships. I always felt like one day I would forgive those who hurt me in the past. I always knew that I wanted to get over what it was that I was feeling. Whether it was betrayal, toxic relationships, or abuse – I knew I wanted to get past the hurt and move on to a brighter future. I heard that forgiveness was me. Therefore, it was my responsibility to forgive and to heal. It was not the job of the other person. This also doesn't mean that *your* act of forgiving means that they will apologize. It doesn't mean that what they did was ok. It is simply for you. It's to help you move forward. Have you ever told someone, "I forgive you," but you honestly didn't? You said the words but they didn't come from a genuine place. They didn't come from a pure heart. They were just empty words. Once I found out that forgiveness was for me and not the other individuals, change happened. Internally, I shifted. That was my moment of change. I knew that I didn't want to be bitter and angry anymore and I understood that forgiveness was a process I needed to go through.

Holding unforgiveness in your heart becomes like poison to your body. It can become toxic to your body. I knew it was time to no longer hold on to resentment and offenses of others. Forgiveness is a process and I was willing to start. I held grudges and bitterness for way too long. My mom passed away over twenty years ago, but I was still angry at her for abandoning us. It was time to surrender it all to God through prayer with the help of the Holy Spirit. I truly believed that God would help me through it all.

When I look back, I can see what shifted me. First, it was choosing salvation. It was choosing to believe that Jesus died for me and that I was forgiven. So, I would say it's my walk with Christ that has truly shifted my life. The word of God has definitely helped me to understand the true meaning of forgiveness. Here are a few scriptures:

Ephesians 4:32 (NLT) – "Instead, be kind to each other, tenderhearted, forgiving one another, just as God through Christ has forgiven you."

Matthew 6:14-15 (NLT) – "If you forgive those who sin against you, your heavenly Father will forgive you. But if you refuse to forgive others, your Father will not forgive your sins."

Matthew 18:21-22 (NLT) – "Then Peter came to him and asked, 'Lord, how often should I forgive someone who sins against me? Seven times?' 'No, not seven times,' Jesus replied, 'but seventy times seven!'"

I've read books on forgiveness. There's one in particular that has inspired me and encouraged me to forgive. The name of the book, written by Pastor Ricardo Manuel, is *Forgiving the Unrepentant.* This book touched me so deeply and taught me to understand that forgiveness was for me and not the other person. I've tried therapy, which was very helpful. It allowed me to dig deep and bring those issues to the surface. All roads of rejection and abandonment led to the roots of unforgiveness.

Have you ever had to forgive someone who was no longer here on earth? They were already deceased, but yet you had to forgive so you could move forward. This is what I struggled with for over a decade. It felt freeing and rewarding in the end.

Ask yourself what was your turning point? In 2018 was mine, I would say. My pastor preached on forgiveness often. His sermons and his book have impacted my decision to forgive those who have wronged me in the past. His book taught me many lessons on forgiveness. I thank God that I met him and that he was the author of a book I needed. A book that would shift my thinking and help me on my journey of forgiveness. God knew exactly why he connected us in that elevator in 2018 in Fayetteville, North Carolina.

I definitely went through a process to get here, to feel this type of peace after forgiving myself and others. Knowing that forgiveness is for me, I understood that I needed it in order to move forward. Moving forward produced a life of peace, joy, and love without bitterness. It released me from being angry and holding resentment towards people who have wronged me in the past. I did not want to live like that anymore and I thank God for His word and grace. I thank God for the scriptures that have held me up. When Jesus told Peter that he was to forgive his brother a limitless number of times, the scripture translates it to 70 x 7 times. This is found in Matthew 18:21-22.

So, not only do I practice forgiving quickly and as often as the scripture says, but I have also forgiven *myself* 70 x7 times. I refuse to live in the offenses of others towards me. I forgive *me* and all that I have done to me. Taking my power back is my responsibility. I choose healing. I am forgiven, and I will live in that truth.

Here's the part where it gets tough. This is a demonstration. I remember doing this myself a few times and it has helped me. Have you ever looked at yourself in the mirror and said the words "I forgive me" to the person you see? Are you ready for this pivotal moment? Are you ready to live free? Are you ready to make that shift? If you are, I want to challenge you today:

Look yourself in the mirror and say these words:
"I forgive me!"

Now, take it a little further. What do you need to forgive yourself of? Have you been living in your past failures? Your mistakes? Your uncompleted goals? Are you stuck in those unfulfilled dreams, the degree you didn't earn, or the time you wasted? What about the job you didn't get, the position you did not qualify for, or the career you didn't choose? What about the books you didn't write, the weight you didn't lose, the college you didn't go to, the accolades you didn't receive? Let's go there. Let's confront the failed relationships, the credit score you didn't reach, the money you wasted. Think about it. Are you living in the past? If so, it's time to move forward. Your best days are ahead.

This is your pivotal moment. Be warned – it may not be easy, but don't stop. If the tears start rolling because you can't get the words out, it's ok. Just don't stop. Look at yourself in the mirror and start the process of forgiving yourself out loud.

These are examples designed to help you think and create your own list. The time is now, forgiveness is for you. It is time to throw that dark blanket off your head. It is time to forgive yourself and heal. It is time for you to walk in your freedom, to walk into forgiveness. God wants to heal you from unforgiveness. No more shame, guilt. *I forgive me...*

I forgive me for allowing myself to not show up for me.
I forgive me for my past mistakes.
I forgive me for all of my failures.
I forgive me for having insecurities.
I forgive me for allowing bitterness to live inside my heart.
I forgive me for allowing other people to make me feel bad about myself.
I forgive me for comparing myself to others.
I forgive me for allowing distractions to hinder my growth.

I forgive me for losing my drive and motivation.

I forgive me for putting others before myself.

I forgive me for allowing Satan to steal my joy.

I forgive me for believing for others and not believing it can be done for me.

I forgive me for allowing people to mishandle me.

I forgive me for prioritizing work over my family time.

I forgive me for not believing who God says that I am.

I forgive me for not taking care of myself mentally, physically, and emotionally.

I forgive me for showing up for everybody else and not showing up for me.

I forgive me for overextending myself for those who did not deserve me.

I forgive me for being my worst critic and bashing myself.

I forgive me for allowing other people's problems to become my own.

I forgive me for not creating boundaries and missing deadlines.

I forgive me for not holding myself accountable.

I forgive me for believing the lies that Satan has told me.

I forgive me for staying in toxic relationships much longer than I needed to.

I forgive me for allowing people to dim my light.

I forgive me for allowing procrastination to cripple my movement.

I forgive me for holding on to people that God released in my last season.

I forgive me for apologizing for things I have not done.

I forgive me for dimming my light to allow others to be comfortable.

I forgive me for all my unhealthy habits and poor choices.

I forgive me for not believing God's promises for my life.

I forgive me for burning bridges God sent to help me.
I forgive me for abandoning God's assignment.
I forgive me for not being a man or woman of my word.
I forgive me for not prioritizing me and loving on me properly.

Decide to take your life back, take your power back, God is not done with you yet. Forgive YOURSELF because God has already forgiven you. It's in His word. Now it's your turn.

My question to you is this: When destiny calls will you answer?

About the Author – Tyshana Mabry-Diaz

Tyshana N. Mabry-Diaz, born and raised in Harlem, NY, is the third child of Tawuana Y. Mabry and Tyrone E. Watson. After losing her mother and oldest sister, Tyshana turned her pain into purpose, pursuing a degree in Human Services from Touro College. She graduated cum laude in 2011, becoming a positive role model for her daughters.

In 2010, she accepted Christ as her Savior and joined Mount Calvary Holy Church under Bishop Michael Yelverton. After college, she worked as a Caseworker and Job Developer at Lutheran Social Services. In 2012, Tyshana's family relocated to Fort Bragg, NC, due to her husband's military career. There, she dedicated herself to supporting her family and community.

Inspired by her desire to give back, Tyshana became an advocate for women in domestic violence situations, partnering with organizations in NC and AZ to provide beauty products to survivors. She has been active in Domestic Violence Awareness Month for seven years.

In 2018, the Diaz family moved to Arizona, where Tyshana was baptized and joined Victory Outreach Mesa. She answered her call to ministry, becoming a licensed preacher in 2020 and was ordained as an Evangelist and Pastor of F.I.G.H.T. Global Ministries in 2022.

As the Founder and President of FGM, Tyshana is committed to sharing the love of Jesus and leading others from crisis to Christ living. She is a Holy Ghost-filled believer, passionate about her assignment to encourage others to live a Christ-centered life.

CHAPTER 7 – TARA MELVIN-MACK

The Coat, the Chair, and the Cave: Moments That Changed Me

Introduction
For you have been my hope, Sovereign LORD, my confidence since my youth. Psalm 71:5 NIV

Before I describe what will become the most interesting season of my church experience, I must offer some context into my life. I am a church girl, period. I can't remember a time in my life when I was not involved in some aspect of church - I even attended a daycare program sponsored by a church from ages 2 to 5 years old. I am familiar and have been taught church protocol, church hymns, church functions - all things church. From Missionary Baptist to Disciples of

Christ to United Holiness to COGIC and Apostolic/Non-Denominational; you name it, I know something about them all. I am familiar with early morning prayer and late-night musicals - even an event or program pertaining to church at least four out of the seven days was not uncommon. Sunday School on Sunday mornings, Intercessory Prayer on Tuesday night, Bible Study on Wednesday night, Choir Rehearsals on Thursday night, Friday night revivals, and Saturday rehearsals/bake sales/yard sales or missionary work in the community became my norm.

I often reflect on my childhood and church experiences and I think of my paternal grandmother, Rosa Butler Melvin, who was instrumental in my musical abilities. I started singing at the age of 4 in the Youth Choir. To be honest, I did not want to be in the choir because I was shy and didn't like singing in front of people. Of course, my mother and family were not having that, so in the choir I went. My grandmother Rosa, who had a piano and an organ in her home, heard me tinkling on the keys from time to time and told my mom that she should sign me up for piano lessons. As a child, I already felt that my time was too consumed in the prayer room and in church, but I did not have any say in the final decision, especially being only seven years old. I started piano lessons while in elementary school, but I had such difficulty reading music. My piano teacher, the late Mrs. Dorothy Johnson from Roseboro NC, knew that I had an ear for music and she helped to cultivate that while teaching me music theory.

Every Tuesday, I had music lessons before bible study at church - I enjoyed it so much that my mother and grandmother added another day to my already busy week. I can remember assisting my grandmother during the summer months while being on break from school. At that time, we did not use typewriters - I had to write the songs (from listening to the radio or cassette player) that my grandmother would teach the church choirs week after week. Rehearsals were typically every Thursday evening and in preparation for those rehearsals, my grandmother would go to the church and practice EVERY song on the organ and piano (now mind you, she had these same instruments at home). After many years of this routine during the summer, I asked her why it was important to go to the church and practice music before the actual rehearsal? Her answer was that the sound is different at home than in the sanctuary and honestly, she wanted to get into the presence of God for herself before inviting others to go with her. Wow - my young mind did not understand it all then, but after a few years as a young musician starting from age 13, it made sense. It is impossible to invite others to experience a place that you have not been. Thank you, Grandma, for that and so many other lessons in my childhood. As an adult, I understand now and I have no regrets about my childhood as I was raised in the admonition of Christ - and the ways of the church. Honestly, my childhood church experiences prepared me for my future experiences in ministry.

The Coat: The Growth That Changed Me

Here is my servant whom I have chosen, the one I love, in whom I delight; I will put my Spirit on him, and he will proclaim justice to the nations.
Matthew 12:18 NIV

I must offer you a glimpse into the beginning of a remarkably interesting leadership journey that started in 2013. I honestly did not know what to expect that day after receiving a call to attend a meeting at church. On a bright, sunny Saturday filled with blue skies and plans to relax and regroup for the week, I jumped in my car and headed to church as the request sounded urgent. Thankfully, I had already showered, got dressed and prepared myself to run some errands, but this "meeting" was not on my task list. While driving through traffic and listening to the radio, a song by Donald Lawrence filled the airwaves. Although I listened to the song playing, my spirit locked into one particular phrase that as I think about it now, was eerily prophetic: "You ain't, seen nothing; you ain't seen nothing yet." ...If I knew then what I know now, I would have allowed that phone call to go straight to voicemail.

I drove into the parking lot and noticed a few other cars parked near the church. I got out of my car and walked slowly into the church not knowing what to expect. This feeling was different than anything I have felt prior to any "rehearsal "or meeting I have had before - somehow deep in my soul I knew that my life was getting ready to change. I walked in through the vestibule and into the cafe area and saw large three-ring binders on tables with names and images of tricycles. This was a moment for me - I did not panic but I was not overly excited about the view that represented a new journey for me. I sat down at the table where the three-ring binder with my name on it was placed and I waited on further instructions. The senior leader walked out of his office and said, "Good morning and welcome to M.I.T. - which stands for 'Ministers in Training' class."

I will describe the last decade and a half of my life as my "coat" season. Typically, coats are used to cover and accessorize the body. Coats are necessary for protection and warmth. Also, if we think of animals, coats represent GROWTH that protects their body from external elements. (Let's keep the latter thought in mind). During this journey of life, I had to put on a new coat in which the responsibilities that I had to grow into both spiritually and naturally were great. In reflection, I was in ministers-in-training, I served as the praise and worship leader/coordinator, keyboardist, and I was a member of the intercessory prayer team. All of these responsibilities afforded me a seat as a secondary leader and a "bridge builder" between membership and senior leaders. While I did not ask to be placed in any of these positions, I knew that God's will for my life included leading in ministry and in music. (*One thing I have learned is that God's purpose and plan for one's life will prevail, no matter how fast one may try to run in the opposite direction of the call.*). If I could take a moment and offer any wisdom to someone who feels the call of God on their life, I would say that building a lifestyle of prayer and fasting would help prepare for the spiritual warfare that will be encountered. Any assignment that is done for or on behalf of God requires prayer! Please understand that you cannot lead, teach, minister, sing, or be a good Christian disciple without disciplining the spirit through prayer and fasting.

It was also during this experience as a secondary leader that I learned the most about myself as a person. I have never claimed to be a perfect person or leader, but I found myself always placing ministry and other people's needs first in front of my own. While it is honorable and admirable to make sacrifices for God's business, if we are not careful, we will find ourselves in seasons of frustration and burnout. For the first couple of years, I enjoyed serving in ministry and doing one of the things that I am called to do, which is teaching. As a praise and worship leader, I was responsible for teaching lyrics, voice parts in songs, and biblical knowledge about the songs. It was important to me that the worship department grew in knowledge and grace in the Word, while having the responsibility of leading others through worship to God during each worship experience. While doing the work of ministry and pleasing others, I was growing and drowning at the same time. I was drowning in ministry because I was trying to maintain two jobs, school, and work to serve a leader who found something wrong in most of the things I did. I will admit that I was not the best organizer and, at times, procrastination was a real enemy for me; but I excelled the most in music and creativity. I wasn't the best administratively as a leader, but I was relational, and I knew how to bring people together for any event that the church planned. For many years, the journey in leadership was rocky because I didn't feel understood or considered. One day, it all came to a boiling point and, despite my best efforts, I found myself sitting in the chair - the first seat on the front row.

The Chair: The Season That Changed Me

But in that coming day no weapon turned against you will succeed. You will silence every voice raised up to accuse you. These benefits are enjoyed by the servants of the Lord; their vindication will come from me. I, the Lord, have spoken!
Isaiah 54:17 NLT

I remember vividly the Sunday that shifted my entire life - October 6, 2019. After a few months of battling anxiety, panic attacks, and anxiety-induced health issues, it happened - the leadership meeting that catapulted my life into a different direction. I will not disclose the details of that meeting, but when it was over, I walked out of the meeting pale, heart racing and feeling as if all life had left me. When a senior leader expresses their disdain for you and says that they no longer want to hear you sing or preach again, especially when they were regarded as a spiritual father, it is soul shattering. So many thoughts raced through my head, but at that moment, I had to hold it together. I had to walk into a church with smiling parishioners ready to worship, yet I'm sitting on the front row after being rebuked and embarrassed in front of my leadership peers. Nothing in my life could have prepared me for that moment – I had never been talked to like that before by anyone in authority, and for it to come from someone I held in high regard...

I sat on the first seat on the front row, in my clergy attire, watching the praise and worship team that I had taught and practically built, worship and move forward WITHOUT me. Anything and anyone can move forward in the absence of a leader or person instrumental to process, so let us not assume that everything stops because one person is not there. To sit there and process that I am not singing lead or background, teaching, or ministering was so overwhelming at that moment. It was overwhelming that seeking therapy was my next step of action. My voice was not silenced in death, but for ninety days, I was not allowed to do anything in that church or anywhere else. In that time, I had a chance to reflect on my non-administrative ways and figure out what the next steps for my life would be. After ninety days of sitting, I found that singing wasn't a passion anymore - if I be honest, ministry really wasn't either. I heard that ninety days forms a lifestyle, so being silent in ministry and not allowed to "operate" outside of that place became a lifestyle. I want to be clear that I never lost my love and faith in God, but ministry was once a sore spot in my heart and soul. I dedicated so much of myself into ministry but because my abilities were misunderstood and misplaced as a leader, it seemed as if I were no longer valuable. I know that was the trick of the enemy to abort the assignment that God had placed in my life, but at the time, that's what I felt. It's funny how one experience can leave you in a bad, triggered place if you don't pull on Holy Spirit to help get you beyond that point. The wounds ran deep, but God's love lifted me from that place where I am able to stand again and allow God to use me in that place and beyond.

The Cave: What Did I Discover in My Time of Obscurity

In his kindness God called you to share in his eternal glory by means of Christ Jesus. So, after you have suffered a little while, he will restore, support, and strengthen you, and he will place you on a firm foundation. All power to him forever! Amen.
1 Peter 5:10-11 NLT

The year 2020 sent all of us home to sit, rethink, reshape, and repattern how we did everything. Our country was in a full pandemic and crisis, and yet my mind and heart were full of peace. The season of sitting caused ministry invitations to cease and my phone/inbox to go silent. While in the cave of obscurity, I had time to reflect on my actions as a person and leader and how I could change to prevent what happened from taking place again. Sitting at home gave me the opportunity to truly seek God and heal from negative emotions and feelings from my chair experience. Wisdom taught me to take care and strengthen what and WHO remains – crying over spilled milk, spilled emotions, deep and intense hurt or words is not beneficial for any situation. How can we minister effectively to those who God is sending our way when our hands are full of the broken pieces of broken relationships and covenants? God heals us from our deepest wounds in order to use us in the most phenomenal ways. I knew while I was in my quiet place with God that I would recover and heal from that situation because my recovery is vital for someone else's journey. There is treasure in the cave if we seek to discover it. In almost forty-five years of living, the peace that I had while fighting back to get to the place of wholeness is immeasurable. The season of the chair broke me in ways that I will never be able to articulate. I will not blame the church for the hurt that happened there – I will not give the devil that much credit. Sometimes, people unknowingly can be used to wreak havoc in our lives that may be hard to recover from without prayer, fasting, therapy, and support. Each season had to take place for me to be who I am today. I preached a sermon a few years ago entitled, "It Made Me Cry, But It

Didn't Make Me Quit!" Whew - that just blessed me again. LOL! I cried in it, but I didn't quit. I took some darts that injured me, but thanks be unto God, they didn't kill me. I heard my name in more conversations than necessary, but I kept smiling and remained faithful. God kept me through it all and I am so grateful. The same God with the same grace can keep you too if you trust Him and His plan. God bless the reader of this chapter and this book - may your heart be healed, restored and forever trust in the God who is able to keep you. AMEN.

About the Author - Tara Melvin-Mack

Tara Mack is a wife, minister of the Gospel, and well known psalmist from Clinton, NC. She is the Executive Pastor of *4 His Purpose Ministries Int'l* and is a proud Fayetteville State University Alumna. She is currently pursuing a Master's Degree in Education from Grand Canyon University and works in Student Affairs Administration at her alma mater, FSU. She is married to Ibadan Mack and they reside in Fayetteville, NC.

CHAPTER 8 – KRIS-SHAE MCCALL

I Can See Clearly Now: The Journey to Becoming

Have you ever felt so lost, disappointed, and off track that you no longer recognized yourself? You look in the mirror and tears begin to fall down your face. You stare and look, after a while, you quicken and move away or lower your head because you wonder, "Why me? How did I get here?" I was asking questions like, "God, how is it possible that You can still love me? I don't even know who I am right now, and You love me?"

Reflecting a little on the meaning of a couple of words, the first word is *see*. To see is to become aware of something, or to recognize. Another definition states to come to know or discover. Think about that for a moment - to become aware and to discover.

Let's break down the definition of clear, it's important for you to have this revelation with me. Clear, having many definitions, I liken to these; easily visible, free from ambiguity, capable of sharpness, and free from doubt. So, in other words, to describe what happened – I became aware and came to know (without a doubt) who I was and my purpose.

My friends, let me tell you this. It brought me to absolute tears while experiencing a myriad of emotions. Here is what I mean; I was relieved to know that I was still loved and I was relieved to receive clarity. I was grateful that I was still chosen for such a time as this and that I have all I need within me to do what I am called to do. Yet, I was also disappointed at myself that I ever felt lost and in such a state of distraction. When this happens, you realize it's time to cry out and ask God for help – in only a way that He can. "Please help me understand. Why am I here? How did I get to this place? How could I allow myself to be here, in this place?" This was, indeed, a place of confusion, sadness, consistent disappointment, and not recognizing myself.

Before I began my journey to becoming, and my personal path to clarity, I thought my life was good. I believed I was successful to a point where my parents were proud of me, and my family recognized I had a few accomplishments and accolades. However, at some point, I almost felt like I was a fraud. It felt like my outward appearance showed that I was successful, happy, at peace, and living in joy. To some extent, I was. However, it wasn't a complete truth. I felt like I was a fraud because something was off internally and I was unfulfilled.

Self-Love

I finally got to the point of questioning myself. What is missing? Why do I feel like something is off? Am I showing myself love? Let's be honest. Many of us *chant* "self-love" and "I love me," but do we really? Remember that love is an action word. Love is in the actions we take day in and day out. Do your actions show that you love yourself? Personally, I was saying that I did, but my behaviors and actions frequently did not align with that statement. Do you know where I'm coming from, or is it just me?

I continued to reflect on it more and more and realized self-love is more than words and it's not an automatic act. We have catchy sayings like "can't nobody love me like me" or "self-love is the best love." These are true; however, when we take time to reflect on how we treat ourselves, how we let others treat us, and what behaviors we accept from others - we may not like what we see. Assessing these things helps show us a true reflection of our level of self-love. Also recognizing we can actively show that we love ourselves, which ultiimately teaches others how to treat us. Walking these things out shows more about our level of self-love than any words that could ever be spoken out of our mouths.

On this journey, a disappointing revelation occurred. I realized I didn't love myself as much as I *said* I did. It was life changing, shocking, hurtful, and disappointing to arrive at this reality. Real talk, it was absolutely necessary to get to that point because I was then able to begin taking inventory of my life. I looked around and, honestly, I didn't like what I saw. I realized that my self-love tree wasn't bearing much fruit. You may be wondering how I was able to recognize that or what that looks like. Let me share some of the things I thought through with you. If any of these resonate with you, it's okay to shake your head in agreement or raise your hand (with a *"yes sis"* in your spirit): *After honest reflection, it meant that I had allowed people to have access to me who did not earn it and who did not show that they honored and valued me.*

Here are a few examples from an **external** perspective:
- People consistently not keeping their word to me, yet I don't address it
- Staying at a job longer than my value was appreciated
- Saying yes to people who consistently let me down
- Dealing with people who are takers and rarely look for an opportunity to give back to me

Let's look at some examples from an **internal** perspective:

- Not sharing my accomplishments with others
- Inconsistent physical activity
- Unhealthy eating habits
- Inconsistent prayer life and meditation
- Negative self-talk

It became resoundingly clear that I had been a poor steward of my body from the inside out. The grace that had been gifted to me offered me time to pull things together, showing my body appreciation and gratitude for the work it does each and every day.

Declare this with me:

I will be a better steward consistently and faithfully over the gifts, talents, abilities, and body I have been blessed to have.

Going through this experience brought so many tears during the process of reflection. However, this had to happen for me to get to my current state of mind. Even as I am writing this, I'm teary eyed with gratitude because I finally got it. I know, I know, I know - my life and your life may not be perfect. But guess what? When you get it, you *get* it and you've *got* it! It's not about perfection; it's about the journey. It's key to focus on what's in front of you. It's about learning, it's about discovery, and about who we become along the way.

Evolve or Die

Thinking back, it would have been great to know how to be okay with change and give myself permission to evolve. Evolution is something that is inevitable for people who want to live on purpose and with purpose. It's about what we do in the process of evolution that really dictates our outcome and who we become. I say evolving is inevitable and it's important because without it, we will die. I mean death by lack of growth, death by not challenging ourselves, death by contentment, death by mediocrity. If we decide to be content and not evolve, we limit our options. Who is with me and realizes where there are limited options, there is limited mobility? You feel stuck and don't see the possibilities of getting out. In those times, bitterness can set in, which is a distressing place to settle into the mind.

When I think about a bitter place, there's really no accountability there. When in a place of bitterness, we tend to blame others for what isn't working. We then create a mental list of what would be better, what happened to us, how much farther in life we'd be if certain things hadn't happened to us, and the list goes on. We declare that we would have better relationships and these emotions can take us even further downhill. Fill in the blank with whatever may be applicable for you. When we choose to be okay with evolving, that means we learn something along the way. There is an *aha* moment that has to occur which causes us to ponder if we should pivot and do something differently. Evolution is the nourishment we need on our journey to becoming who we're meant to be and reaching our full potential. A critical key in the process of evolving is that you don't need validation from anyone else. Not man, not woman, not anyone. You don't have to check in with others unless you decide that you need an accountability partner. You're learning, you're growing, you're stretching, and your purpose is in front of you. You begin to see it; even when it looks fuzzy, it's there. Even when it's cloudy and it's raining hard with life's trials and hardships, so hard that you can barely see your way, it's still there. Please understand that you're going to have to throw away the idea of things being just right or having your ducks all in a row. You must throw perfectionism out of the window.

I'm going to take a moment to share a story with you. I will pause here to say I had never considered myself a perfectionist; however, the power of discovery and insight is a beautiful gift. I was in a coaching session in 2021 and one of the things she let me know was that she saw me. I mean truly saw me. She observed a key aspect of who I was and this is what she said:

"You come to your sessions, and you have your laptop, you have your notes, you've completed your assignment, and you're all ready to go. I see that you are very organized, and it is clear that you have a level of excellence in the things that you do."

A key insight she was sure to articulate to me clearly is when she said to me, " *Your good is someone else's great.*" When she said that to me, I had to take a moment to let it sink in and process it. While she saw me processing, she looked at me and said, "Hear me again. *Your good is someone else's great.*"

What she meant by that was my tendency to change, tweak, or perfect "a thing" before I make it available to anyone else was hindering me and slowing me down. She said, "I want you to be okay with your 80% because your 80% - I promise you - is better than a lot of people's 100%." I had to sit back and think about that for a moment. To be honest with you, even though I did take time to reflect on it at that moment, it is still something I reflect on to this day. It is one of the things that serves as a catalyst for me to accelerate and stop sitting on an action when I need to execute. After further discovery, I was actually using perfectionism as a method of procrastination and delay when I was afraid and uncomfortable doing something new and outside of my norm. If this is you, I encourage you to release the thinking that something has to be perfect. Our growth comes in the action, the actual doing of a thing. The healing comes while doing it. Yes, that thing that's sitting on the shelf, desk, or table waiting for you to pick it back up and complete it. That's where your healing lies. Catch that please and understand that healing and deliverance comes while *doing* the action. We are blessed and bless others as we overcome the challenges that have stifled us and move into action. Even with this new awareness, I didn't quite understand the extent of what she was saying, so it was hard for me to execute with a level of expeditiousness needed to get certain things done. This usually only applies to things that are for my personal development, personal growth, or entrepreneurial growth. I execute for others with no problem at all. Raise your hand if I'm not the only one. We can often move at a level of precision and expediency for someone else. However, when it comes to us moving personally, we don't always do right by ourselves. To be honest, that's still a challenge at times. Yes, I am still on the journey to becoming better and wondering why I have such a hard time doing something for me than I do for other people. You remember earlier we talked about self-love, right? The key is now I can recognize it quicker and I know how to stop going down the negative sinkhole. Something that helps me that you can try is taking the negative thoughts and questions and turning them into positive statements. Do I not believe that I'm worth it? (I believe I'm worth it.) Do I not believe that I deserve to put forth all my own effort, focusing on something important to me and a part of my purpose? (This is important to me and I deserve 100% effort and focus.)

I would also tell myself to go big or go home. "Baby girl, step out of the fog." I am literally smiling and crying at the same time while I'm writing this because it means so many things as I reflect on my life. What I mean by "go big or go home" is that you already know you don't do anything halfway. You weren't raised that way as a child. Mediocrity is unacceptable; but somehow - when it comes to things that you say are important, or when it comes to things that feed you, grow you, improve you, make you better, or will cause you to excel - you don't follow the philosophy of "go big or go home." My friends when I say this, I'm talking about everything, baby! Do it all! If you want to position yourself to attract more coins, do so. If you desire to grow spiritually, focus in and do that. Dig in and go full throttle. Don't compromise your values, your morals, your purpose, or your personal integrity. If you want to be in better health, commit to yourself. Figure out what that means, practice consistency, and find your way through it. Decide to be the best *you* that you've envisioned.

Lastly, give yourself grace. Every day is not a day you will do the thing you thought you would. Every day is not a day you will get the outcome you thought you would get. Every day is not a day that you will receive the love that people promised they would give and show you. Every day is not a day you will see what you believe. Every day is not a day that you will trust what you see. Every day is not a day that you will always want to commit to the sacrifice it takes to reach the goal you've set. But still, you've got to get up and show up - every single day!

The Turning Point

Now let me ask you this: have you experienced a turning point? A moment that caused you to make a significant change? A moment in which you had a realization that "something" had to be done now? "If I don't do this now, if I don't start this journey now, if I don't leave this place now, and change, I will surely die." You may think that sounds a bit dramatic. I assure you that if a significant change is necessary in your life and you don't *do* something in response to it to turn in a different direction, you will die. You will slowly become unrecognizable to yourself. It may be a specific characteristic that used to be important but would no longer be. It might be a dream or goal you used to have that would no longer be, or a value you used to cherish that may slowly wither and no longer hold weight in your life. If you've ever had a moment like that, what did you do? At that moment, did you have all the answers you needed to make that significant change? Could you foresee the challenges that would come because you made that significant change? I dare say that you didn't have all the answers because the process simply doesn't work like that. You must have a level of faith and believe there is purpose and significance for that change and what it means for your life. From that moment on, if you believe that, you will begin to put one foot in front of the other and walk it out. You begin to go forward, not knowing exactly what it means, but you just go because what you *do* know is "if I don't begin, I will die." You may be thinking what could possibly be at risk of dying? These are a few things I knew were at risk for me: purpose, passion, self-worth, endurance, and my motivation.

Continuing to think about my turning point, a song title comes to mind. Specifically, the award-winning song by Anita Baker titled *Giving You the Best That I Got.* I'm talking about extended hours, best ideas, sacrifice, intellectual capital, money, and dedication. There is certainly nothing wrong with having the heart of a giver. There is nothing wrong with how you are created to be if you are a true giver. The key for us is to exercise discernment, understanding, and balance. When we do not exercise these things it leaves us with an empty cup and nothing left to pour. Do you understand what I mean? Take a guess what was left for me after giving so much of myself.

Simply put, not much at all. I'm telling you I was giving the best of myself to everyone *except* me. After all, I thought that was what it took, that it was what was necessary, and that's what everybody did to show up as successful in any area. It didn't leave much for me to feed my purpose, feed my heart's desires, or feed my relationships with others. Certainly, it didn't leave me much to feed and nourish myself spiritually, emotionally, or mentally. I finally realized that when I was living with an empty cup, I began to be easily frustrated and couldn't figure out why. I wasn't able to put my finger on the problem right away. It was sometimes the least little thing that would be an interruption to the way I had my day planned that would cause great frustration. It could be an urgent email that would cause me to have to scratch my plans and make changes to my action list for the day. Mind you, I am the type of person that plans the next day the day before. Let me tell you this type of impromptu call to action and disruption could really rock my world. I am an action driven individual so when I thought I would be able to focus on specific priorities and a major shift was necessary, frustration would set in. The act of shifting everything around was truly frustrating.

One day, I literally had to pause and ask myself why this situation was bothering me so badly. Why was I so frustrated, and so much, by this? The skill of adaptability is key to having success in my profession and it had been common practice for me so it was truly concerning for me at this moment. I consider myself to be a solutionist and normally, this type of opportunity would ignite me, causing me to act urgently to orchestrate a solution. I would do whatever was necessary to bring a swift and effective resolution to meet the current need. My level of self-awareness had begun evolving at this time, and I had my turning point. I became aware that I was compromising. I was compromising my self-worth, value proposition, and purpose because of comfort and fear. I was sitting too comfortably in the seat of mediocrity and was being shifted and unsettled for a while, and finally the frustration of it all came.

At this moment the pivot of my life started, I began a new path to strengthening my self-worth, living out the actions of self-love, seeking out the knowledge to improve my health, and intentionally working to be the woman I am destined and purposed to be. This has been a daily commitment of creating new habits, letting my light shine unapologetically, living in the present, setting and enforcing boundaries, and releasing things that I do not have the power to control.

I have some questions for you. I really want you to take some time to think about them and answer them honestly. Is there anything stopping you from seeing clearly? What has to happen to cause your moment of pivot? What will you do when you hear your destiny crying out for you? Will you hear it? Will you recognize it?

My Prayer For You:

I pray that your eyes be open, your heart be open, and that you listen with your heart so you can be led with confidence and clearly see your destiny. I pray that you will follow the path that is laid out for you and move forward unapologetically. See yourself fulfilling your destiny and move forward one step at a time. Go in confidence, go in peace, go in certainty, and always go with God.

About the Author – Kris-Shae McCall

Kris-Shae McCall, MHA, RHIA, CHPS is a lover of life

and leadership who enjoys serving the community. She is a speaker, coach, certified Maxwell Leadership trainer, business owner, and mentor on a mission to help women lead and live in their authenticity.

For over fifteen years, she's been a sought-after strategy and solution architect. Kris-Shae aspires to create a generation of equipped, confident leaders because she knows the struggle of what it's like to not have a mentor and coach there to support you as you create and implement leadership strategies. In 2019 she began the process of mentorship and training with Maxwell Leadership Certified Team, which seeded the creation of Without Walls Professional Development, LLC. Her approach is to partner with clients promoting the discovery in the power of using their strengths to lead in such a way that will positively impact, inspire, and influence those they lead for years to come.

In 2020 Kris-Shae successfully completed a long-term goal and became a licensed real estate broker in North Carolina. This has provided an opportunity for her to serve the community in an exciting and different capacity. Kris-Shae states "Being trusted to walk along side of someone each step of the way as they make life changing decisions is such an honor. Building a network of trusted colleagues to provide support and simplify real estate transactions for others is an amazing experience." She gladly serves the communities in both the Sandhills and Triad Regions of North Carolina.

Whether working with clients, leading her team, or volunteering, others are drawn to her authenticity, kindness, and compassion. She is known for leaving her imprint on others through her positivity and encouragement.

THE MOMENT OF CHANGE: WHEN DESTINY CRIED AND I ANSWERED

CHAPTER 9 – TASHANA HOWARD

Embrace Your Kairos Season

The act of "being okay" in the current season in which you are in can be difficult. Especially if you have been in the same season for a very long time. We usually fall into one of two categories during this time in our lives: we either become too comfortable, that when the season finally changes we refuse to move, or we just give up and lose faith that the season will actually change. There are times when seasons overlap, such as winter starts to feel a little like spring and spring can sometimes begin to feel a little like summer, despite the fact that the calendar says otherwise. The important thing to remember is that a season is only temporary, and we must be content and embrace the season in which we are in by changing and adjusting our clothing and footwear.

The biblical meaning of the word Kairos is defined as "God's appointed time to act." Each season of our lives is a Kairos season that God has chosen for us. As a 46 year old single sista, I have been asked the questions, "What are you waiting on to have children? Why are you still single?" My response to the first question has always been, "I do not have children because I want to have children within a marriage," and "I am still single because I am waiting on the purpose partner that God has for me." Not a perfect partner, but a purpose partner. Please do not get it twisted; Tashana, also known as Tee, has not lacked in the area of suitors, but those suitors served their purpose in those seasons of my life and when the time came we both moved on to the next season. If I had my way, of course I would have been married in my 20's or 30's, but that was not God's calling for my life. This is God's appointed time for me to be unmarried and I am okay with this season. It's only temporary. I have spent the past few years of this season drawing closer to God through prayer and reading my word with no interruptions. I have embraced this season by earning additional degrees, making divine connections, traveling wherever I want, and enjoying life with wonderful friends. I refuse to sit still just because I have yet to say, "I do." I will be productive in this single season. If I sit around and complain in this season, how can God trust me to be productive in my married season?

How are you embracing the Kairos season that you are in? This is God's appointed season for you to act. To act means to "take action." Are you taking action in this season or are you just sitting still and complaining? I have never seen where complaining about how cold it is outside has changed the temperature or the season from winter to spring. What can you be doing differently to embrace your current season?

As a child, I was always the person who entertained the younger kids at family functions. I started raising children when I was 12 and 13 years old. I have made bottles, given baths, purchased school clothing, and helped complete financial aid and college applications for children I did not give birth to. Yes I wanted children of my own, and now giving birth is not in the plan for me. I have been, and still am, the best auntie that I can be. My Kairos season did not include me giving birth to children of my own. Instead, God called me to take action as an auntie by pouring into my nieces, nephews, and cousins through prayer and God's wisdom (even though the older ones sometimes do not want to hear it). My past job as an elementary teacher and my current job as a School Counselor and School Mental Health Support Specialist have allowed me to interact with and pour into children daily.

I've learned that a person does not have to give birth to be a mother figure. What if I had chosen to just sit still, and complain about not being a "biological mom" in this appointed season as an auntie and educator? I would have missed out on the opportunity to provide love and support to children who needed it the most. To the women who are between the ages of 35 and 45, who are asked that silly question all of the time by people who do not know your "why," it's okay sunshine! You may even feel the need to rush things just to have a child. Please don't. If it is meant for you to birth a child then you will; if it is not, that is okay. You will be a mother in God's way and in His timing. Embrace what He is asking you to do in this appointed time and season for the children of others and act on it.

Don't despise the season that you are in right now. Genesis 8:22 reads, "As long as the earth endures, seedtime and harvest, cold and heat, summer and winter, day and night will never cease." Just as the calendar seasons will always change, going through various seasons is a part of life. It is time for you to look at each season of your life as God's appointed time for you to act. Don't be selfish during your Kairos season. If you are unsure as to how to act, seek God and ask Him what He would have you do while going through the seasons that you are in. Yes I said seasons because, as I stated earlier, seasons have the tendency to overlap. During the overlapping of calendar seasons, we must rely on the meteorologist's report to decide what to wear, such as a jacket for the cool mornings and a short sleeve shirt for the warm afternoons. You may be going through more than one tough season during this time. Allow God to be your meteorologist and rely on Him to order your steps during your current seasons. Most of us just love the warmer months but not the cold months as much. You must embrace the happy seasons along with those not so happy ones. God designed them all. Romans 8:28 reads, "And we know that for those who love God, that is, for those who are called according to his purpose, all things are working together for good." The good, bad, and the ugly will work together for your good. All of your seasons were appointed by God, take action!

The way that each calendar season has a purpose so does the seasons of our life.

Winter is known as the season of hibernation. It's cold outside and some states are fortunate enough to get snow during this time. Many get the "winter blues." What is God asking you to do during your winter season? Maybe God wants you to reflect on His goodness during this time and practice self-care. Maybe He wants you to spend more time with family and friends instead of separating yourself.

Spring is known as the season of new beginnings. The sun begins to shine more and the days become longer. Spring also brings some rain, but after the rain the sun quickly shines again. Maybe God wants you to shift into something new during this season of your life. You're comfortable right where you are, but God has more for you to do and it requires you to move out of your comfort zone and into what may be an uncomfortable place. The best thing about uncomfortable places is that God is right there with you. Jeremiah 29:11 reads, "For I know the plans I have for you," declares the Lord "plans to prosper you and not to harm you, plans to give you hope and a future."

Summer is the joyous season. It is the time that we are open to taking adventures with family and friends. We have more energy during this time. It is much warmer during this season which brings mosquitoes, snakes, and other critters. Do not allow pesty folks to steal your joy during this season. John 10:10 reads, "The thief cometh not, but for to steal, and to kill, and to destroy: I come that they might have life, and that they might have *it* more abundantly." This is your appointed time to enjoy the life that God has given you to the fullest.

Autumn is the "slow down" season. There is a chill that enters the air during this season and the leaves begin to change colors. Autumn requires us to add a layer of clothing. Ravaging hurricanes become more evident during this season. As you walk through this Kairos season of your life take a step back and work through your feelings and emotions. Your mental health is so important to God. Sometimes He will "slow us down" long enough to allow us to work through overthinking and to release mental stress.

I have learned to stop limiting God. As a young girl, I recall running around with my older cousins and watching them catch lightning bugs in a jar. Holes were added to the lid and we would watch the lightning bugs fly around within the jar with no way to escape. Sometimes as children of God, we place Christ's abilities in a closed up jar through our negative thinking and actions. We think and say things such as, "I wish that my bank account looked like hers or his." Our fears of completing that job application or failing that certification test keeps us in the same comfortable unhappy place. As kids, after a short while, we would always take the lid off of the jar and allow the lightning bugs to fly free. It's time for you to stop putting God in your own closed jar and allow Him to move freely through your life. The things that God can do for us has no limits.

Ephesians 3:20-21 reads, "Now unto him that is able to do exceeding abundantly above all that we ask or think, according to the power that worketh in us, unto him be glory in the church by Christ Jesus throughout all ages, world without end. Amen." Stop putting limits on God. This is your Kairos season to apply for the job, start the business, go back to school and earn the degree, and claim overflow in your life. The fear that you have is not coming from God, because He said that He will give us more than we can even ask for or think of according to the power that works in us. Release the spirit of comfortability, fear, and negative thinking that is working within you and allow God's spirit of faith, joy, peace, wisdom, and newness work within you. Do not make the mistake of becoming so comfortable in a season that you make it a permanent Kairos season and mistake it for God's will.

March 2024, as I write these very words, God is shifting me into a new Kairos season. Sharing my story has not been comfortable. Writing the very words that you are reading is new to me, but God divinely connected me to my Literary Midwife that pushed me out of my comfort zone and into a space that I have never been before. This is definitely God's appointed time for me, but what if I had chosen not to act? It is my hope that my words will inspire and encourage every person who reads them, but if I had chosen to never put my pen to paper I would never know. This moment is definitely a moment of change for me. Destiny cried out to me saying, "do it and believe," and I had to answer.

I'm not sure what you are feeling during this season of your life. Always remember that every season has its purpose in your life. Many do not like the rain because the sky becomes cloudy and gloomy. It is important to remember that the rain brings water for the land and crops that are needed for growth. The rain also forces us to slow down and sit down, which many times is needed for all of us. I'm a firm believer that rain and thunderstorms bring the best sleep. There are also those times when rain brings a beautiful rainbow, which makes me think of these words that I heard sung by Sam's Spring AME Zion church senior choir as a young girl, "God put a rainbow in the clouds, when it looks like the sun wouldn't shine anymore, God put a rainbow in the clouds." After a hard rain, the sun always shines again if not the same day, it will shine the next day, the sun will shine again and God always keeps his promises.

Whatever season you are currently in, ask God the following questions:

- God, is this You?
- What do You want me to do during this season?
- God, what steps would You like for me to take during this season?
- God, whose life do You want me to touch?
- God, will You give me wisdom during this season?
- God, will You order my steps during this season?
- God, will you draw me closer to You during this season?

It's time for you to believe that God has a purpose for your life and nothing that occurs in your life is by happenstance. This is God's appointed time for you to act. Don't waste this moment just because it doesn't look quite right or because it is a little difficult. Pray and ask God the questions outlined above. Allow Him to answer each question for you while you are in your quiet place. Once He answers, trust Him and believe, and finally "get up and move."

There is a big difference between believing God and believing *in* God. To believe God means to believe what He says is true. To believe in God means to believe that He exists. I feel that a person cannot say they believe God exists, but do not believe that what He says is true. A person cannot have one without the other. To believe that God exists means you believe that His son - Jesus - exists and that every word that He has said is true. Hebrews 11:6 says, "But without faith it is impossible to please Him. For whoever would come near to God must believe that God exists and that He is the rewarder of those who earnestly *and* diligently seek Him." It is time for you to believe that God exists during your winter, spring, and fall seasons, and seek Him. It is also time for you to believe that everything that He has said about you, your health, your finances, your family, and everyone connected to you is true. He is saying today that you and everyone connected to you are healed, blessed in your finances, protected, loved, has peace, joy, and wisdom. He rewards those who diligently seek Him in all areas of life.

Embrace your Kairos season. I promise you that it is God ordained. Just believe!

About the Author – Tashana Howard

Tashana Howard, a native of Roseboro, North Carolina, is a dedicated educator and mental health advocate. She holds a B.S. in Elementary Education and a M.Ed. from Fayetteville State University, plus a M.Ed. in Professional School Counseling from Liberty University. With a deep passion for student success, she has supported learners from Kindergarten through college as an elementary teacher and Professional School Counselor.

Currently residing in Fayetteville, North Carolina, Tashana works as a School Mental Health Support Specialist with Cumberland County Schools and teaches as an adjunct college instructor. In her spare time, she enjoys family, friends, travel, concerts, and community service with Alpha Kappa Alpha Sorority, Inc.®, Rho Omega Omega Chapter.

Her favorite scripture, Jeremiah 29:11, reflects her commitment to guiding students toward a hopeful future: "For I know the plans I have for you," declares the Lord, "plans to prosper you and not to harm you, plans to give you hope and a future."

CHAPTER 10 - SHAUNA MONROE

The Unwavering Strength I Didn't Know I Had

Life can be unfair at times. It is extremely easy to find yourself in situations that may seem cruel. Grief is just one thing a person can experience that can make them feel as if their entire world is crumbling or falling apart. Google defines grief as "deep sorrow caused by someone's death." Oscar award winning actress Regina King is a grieving mother. In a recent *Good Morning America* interview, she stated something that I found to be very profound. She said, "Grief is love that has no place to go." I can understand that sentiment because you once showed a person love daily, and now that person is no longer here. Now what do you do? It almost feels as if you don't know what to do with that love you once shared with that person because they are no longer here in the physical sense to receive it. It hurts so bad to feel that way, and it just does not seem fair. Sometimes people misplace their feelings and emotions after the loss of a loved one or confuse them for something else. Grief can be very confusing. It is difficult to come to grips with the fact that our loved ones are really gone, but even more difficult to fathom the fact they are never coming back. The fact of the matter is that if we truly once loved a person and they only left due to death, we will always love them despite their absence from the body. Our love does not go away just because that person is no longer alive. Misplaced feelings are not as uncommon as people may think during the processing of the five stages of grief. Everyone will process and get through their grief differently and at different rates. No one should be rushed through their grieving process. Their process is just that; their way of processing their own experience. Unfortunately, there are no short-cuts in this process. If you have ever had love and loss in your heart for someone, you will have to grieve that loss.

Death is not the only cause of grief. Any type of loss can be a trigger for grief. Google states that grief is a normal response to any major loss such as the death of a loved one, but grief can also occur when dealing with a long term or terminal illness. You can also experience grief when experiencing the loss of a home, friendship, romantic relationship, job, or a host of other life experiences. Through these different experiences, the loss could impact life significantly, causing you to grieve that loss or how your lives once were or how your lives could have been. It is also possible to grieve the future that never will be. No matter what the cause of your grief is, you will have to find a way to get through the painful, devastating process, where it feels like you are hurting more than healing and struggling to find the light at the end of the tunnel.

Death is surely a part of life because as sure as you are born, you will one day have to die; however, the death of a loved one who is close to you is not something anyone can ever truly be prepared for. Even if your loved one is terminally ill and you know the day is near, you will never be mentally prepared for that moment to come when they leave.

In 2023, I found myself saying, "Oh my God, why me?" My daughter was only 17 years old, and she had to leave me. I was not prepared and I'm not sure if she was either. I did not get the opportunity to say goodbye. I didn't get a chance to get an extra special hug or kiss, to say an extra "I love you," and I will regret that for the rest of my life. I'm not sure if God had a conversation with her before she went with Him. I don't know if He whispered in her ear and gave her a pep talk before it was time for her to go with Him. All I know is that she and I went to bed the night before, everything was fine like any other night, and only one of us woke up the next morning. That was the worst day of my entire life. It was not fair. So, I ask again, "Oh my God, why me?" All I wanted to know at that moment was why was this happening to me?! So, as much as I trust and believe in God and as much as I know that as sure as we live, we also have to die one day, I still want to know why my sweet girl had to go and why God only wanted her to live for 17 years. I want to know why her assignment on earth was completed in a short 17 years. Oh my God, why me?

On that sad day in August of 2023, when I felt like my world had also come to an end, the EMTs uttered the words, "I'm sorry, but there are no signs of life" to me regarding a person that I had given life to. My first reaction was no reaction at all. I just stood there completely blank. I was completely in shock. I was looking at them as if they had made a mistake and needed to go back and try again, after they had already been working for a different outcome for about 30-45 minutes. It just didn't seem like this could be real. They could not have really been saying that to me. I desperately needed this to be a mistake or a bad dream. Was this really happening? Was my child really gone? I fell to the floor, still not saying a word. I could not even fathom the words to say. My daughter lived with autism and her aid was already in route to work with her in the community for the day. Just a few moments later she walked through my front door, saw the first responders, and instantly figured out what was going on. She began screaming and trying to get into my daughter's bedroom. She grabbed me and it was at that moment that I began to believe this was my reality, and I began screaming to the top of my lungs. "Oh my God, why me?" This was the absolute worst day of my entire life. There was no day that could even come close to being as horrible as this day, other than the day I lost my mother. No mother should ever have to endure this type of pain. How do I go on from here? How do I heal from this permanent hole in my heart? Why did my daughter have to leave me? This made absolutely no sense to me. This had to be a dream or something. My mind was having trouble processing what was happening; but in my mind, as my house was filled with people, there was no way this could be real. These were so many thoughts going through my head. My condo was filled with first responders, forensics, medical examiners, detectives, and coroners. It felt like the whole city was there and I was having panic attacks. It felt like the room was spinning. This is when I learned that when someone passes away at home, it is a death-homicide investigation. I didn't know whether to be grateful because they were looking out for the best interest of my child, or humiliated because I felt like I was under investigation. I later spoke with the medical examiner who explained to me the reason for every single part of the investigation, to include the photographs that were taken. She told me that from the investigation, she could tell my daughter had been very well taken care of, and she explained that everything was standard and legal protocol for the protection of my daughter or whoever has passed away. I wanted nothing more than for this all to have been just a bad dream; unfortunately, that was not my reality. At least, after speaking with the medical examiner, I no longer felt like a criminal but a grieving mother. She was a very kind and compassionate person who thoroughly explained the process to me, and she provided her condolences, letting me know that I was not suspected of any wrongdoing. That is actually how I felt prior to speaking with her.

Before my daughter went to Heaven, I prided myself on being a great mother. I was a special needs mother with little to no support. I was never relieved for any breaks, I rarely had people to check on me just to see how I was doing. Outside of working, my child was always by my side. Although I was often tired, I never gave up. I trusted that God would always make a way out of no way for me. I always figured out a way to overcome any obstacle I faced. I was an advocate for my child. I was always the voice she did not have until the very end. I had my mind set on the fact that I would more than likely never be an empty nester. I had one adult child who was a college graduate, out of the home, successful, and doing well for herself. Then, I was also a special needs mom and caregiver to my other daughter who was seventeen. I had become ok with the idea of never being an empty nester and I had mentally prepared myself to be a caregiver for the rest of my days. I could have never imagined being an empty nester in this way.

My daughter was sweet, pure, and innocent. She had challenges in her life and many ailments, but all of her doctors agreed that nothing should have caused death. Imagine how confused this left me. Together, we had gotten through every single obstacle that came our way and now she was gone. I honestly had no clue what to do, how to feel, or even how to breathe. She transitioned to another life, and I transitioned from being speechless and having daily panic attacks to going days and weeks in bed asking God over and over, "Why me?" I became frustrated with God because I felt like I was just not getting the response I desperately needed. I had no idea that I had to go through this involuntary process called grief.

She was only a child, yet her life had come to an end. Never in my life had I felt so stuck in my own thoughts. Although I pride myself on being a good mother, I still wonder if she felt the same. Was I a good mother to her? Does God feel that I had done a good enough job, according to His standards? People tell me all the time how much of a great mom I am, but I just want that confirmation from God and my baby girl, being that she was taken away from me. Grief can make you doubt what you already know to be true or make you become frustrated about what you feel you need confirmation on.

When you experience trauma in the loss of a loved one, even as a Believer, you may call on Jesus while still wondering how He's going to get you through the amount of pain you're feeling. Maybe the perfect people don't feel that way, but I did. I don't consider that to be disbelief in Him. I consider that being real. We can choose to believe God but the pain of losing a child can allow even the biggest Believer to have weak moments. Prayer changes things, so thank God for Jesus. Thank God that He knows our heart on our good days, as well as our bad ones. Hebrews 11:1 says, "*Now faith is the substance of things hoped for, the evidence of things not seen.*" That means to me I believe God can and will do it for me, but the pain is so immense that I just can't understand how He'll be able to. I just believe and trust that He will. I surrender my burdens to Him. All I can do is say, "Lord do it for me," as the song writer says.

When destiny called, I had no choice but to answer. I had to realize that God had equipped me with just enough strength to get through whatever challenges He had placed in my life. Life will always be full of ups and downs and highs and lows. Life is an ongoing cycle. We will never *not* be going through something – as long as we keep on living. Throughout my life, I have experienced challenges that, at times, have been difficult to get through. But somehow, I managed to get through those dark days and find my way to the brighter days, with faith - even when it was only the size of a mustard seed. I encourage all special needs parents to believe that we will survive our circumstances because our help comes from a power that is beyond the help from family, friends, our community, or that any village could ever offer or provide. Our help comes from God, the most reliable source. God is the source that can never disappoint or leave us hanging. Philippians 4:13 says, "*I can do all things through Christ who strengthens me,*" and it is so. God gave me the strength that I needed to keep going because He ordained me to be a parent to my children. He lends our children to us for however long they were meant to be on this earth. He calls us to take on certain tasks in His Kingdom and to perform certain duties in the world. I was created for a purpose, even if I have not completely figured out all that God has for me to do just yet. He would not give us children and not equip us to properly care for them. He would not assign us tasks or duties and not grant us the proper training or etiquette to complete those tasks and duties.

In the moment when destiny called but my pain was stinging and tears were flowing, it was easy for my mind to believe that God had left me hanging and there was no plan. But God promised He'd never leave me or forsake me. Although grief is a process, once you have had a chance to clear your head, breathe, and think clearly, you will eventually be able to see things more clearly. Then the order of things will begin to fall into proper place even more. Traumatizing events can cause brain fog, memory loss, and lack of motivation. It can cause us to be less organized and discouraged; but when you remember who you are in the Lord, there is no stopping you. Destiny has called you to be great no matter what is going on around you. Please answer!

About the Author – Shauna Monroe

Shauna Monroe was born and raised in Fayetteville, North Carolina. She is mom to two daughters. She was an autism mom/caregiver for seventeen years and is now recently an angel mom and learning to adjust to being a grieving mother. Shauna holds a Bachelor of Science in Psychology from Fayetteville State University and a Master of Arts in Family and Marriage Counseling from Liberty University. Shauna currently works in Long Term Care Medicaid and is currently considering making decisions on education and career changes once again now that she has been signed up for a new life. No matter what she decides, giving up is not in the plan!

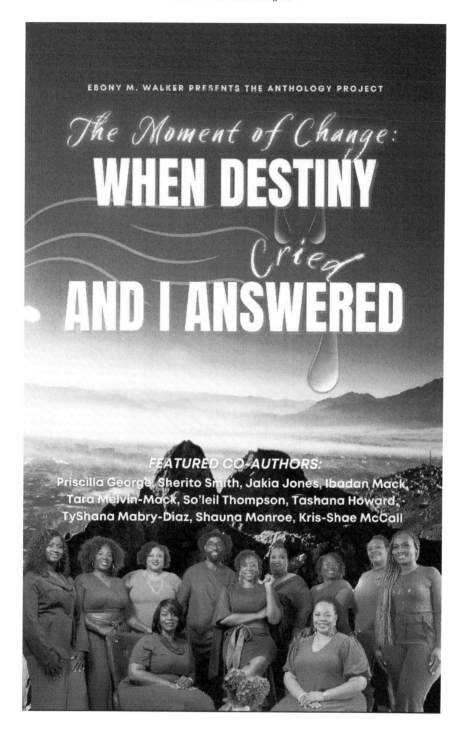

ABOUT THE PROJECT COORDINATOR

Hailing from Moore County, North Carolina, Ebony grew up in Eastwood (Pinehurst area) and defied countless odds. Her life's path has been marked by triumph over challenges that would have deterred many. From surviving molestation and navigating parents' addictions to enduring drug-ridden environments and battling depression, Ebony's story defies grim statistics. Her tenacity thwarted the grip of despair, rewriting a narrative that could have tragically ended in suicide. She accredits God and motherhood with shaping and rerouting her for a greater destiny.

Armed with a degree in Criminal Justice, she embarked on a career as a Paralegal and Professional Background Screener, briefly traversing the legal landscape. Yet her true passions - writing, speaking, and music - beckoned. She finally embraced her writing gifts with newfound seriousness. Today, she stands as the CEO of Walk UpWrite, a platform offering an array of services including ghostwriting, copywriting, and book coaching. Known as *Your Literary Midwife*, her clientele spans continents. She is also the Founder of What's Next Strategy Consulting, helping ministries and business owners create plans of actions that target their next levels of success and attainment.

Ordained as a Pastor in April 2014 and affirmed as a Prophet in August 2024, Ebony has also been recognized as the following: Think Smart 40 Under 40 Recipient, North Carolina Chapter Leader for JNG (Jus' Networking Girlz), Multi Award Winner for ACHI Magazine (2021 Servant Leader of the Year, 2022 Woman of the Year, 2023 Distinguished Service Award), 9x Amazon International Bestselling Author, Future Rich Aunties 2024 Social Impact Award, and more. Her influence extends to the media, with features via ABC, FOX, CBS, NBC, CW, Boston Herald, Telemundo, and the list goes on. She has spoken on stages in front of powerful marketplace figures and has been accredited with resuscitating the visions of millionaires and billionaires. A dynamic keynote and motivational speaker, as well as a sought after panel facilitator and event emcee, Ebony is unashamed of being a woman of prayer. She relies wholeheartedly on God's grace to fulfill her assignments. Her knack for written and spoken communication underscores her life's purpose.

Presently residing in Fayetteville, NC with her husband, John Walker, she is the mother to a blended family of four adult children and ten grandchildren. When not working on a book project, coaching other authors, speaking life into corporate audiences, mentoring young women, or traveling the world doing ministry, Ebony enjoys visiting historical landmarks, attending sporting events, networking, and showing up in the rooms where her gift is needed.

To connect further with Ebony, scan the **QR** code!

Made in the USA
Columbia, SC
13 December 2024